The JOY of JINTIES

The 3F 0-6-0Ts of the LMS and BR, 1924-1967
Part Three 47460-47579

IAN SIXSMITH
Tables by Richard Derry

The fine art of the shunter, man and engine; make their acquaintance again on page 49.

Irwell Press Ltd.

Acknowledgements

Thanks to Allan Baker, Tony Wright, Mike Fell, Peter Groom, Chris Mills, Nick Deacon, Derek Phillips, Tony Sheffield, Paul Chancellor, Mike King and Clive Cottrell. Richard Derry compiled the tables with customary assiduity, wrestling with sometimes arcane recording practices of well over half a century ago. Clive Cottrell teased out of the figures, so far as it is possible, 'incremental' mileages from 'actual' mileages between repairs. The mileages are now 'actual' in that they relate to miles run in the actual period. I'm especially grateful to Clive Cottrell for his efforts. The Joy of Jinties does not extend to the Joy of Jinty Tables – not after several hundred anyway!

I'm particularly grateful to Mr John Jennison for allowing me the freedom of the tirelessly brought together *LMS Locomotive Profiles No.14 Standard Class 3 Freight Tank Engines* (Hunt, Essery and Jennison, Wild Swan Publications 2010).

Cover. Barry Taylor writes: '47535 at Chesterfield, date unknown; sadly the spire just peeping out on the right is not the famously wonky one. The Jinty is some way south of Midland station on the main line in from Derby, etc. – the location is that strange place where three lines crossed. The partly demolished viaduct running across the picture is the old Lancashire, Derbyshire & East Coast Railway (later GC) line from the Lincoln area to Chesterfield Market Place, some way off to the left. Just visible in front of 47535 is the top of a signal on the ex-Manchester Sheffield & Lincolnshire Railway (again, later GC) line from Grassmoor Junction to Chesterfield Central, which runs beneath the lot and then curves north up into town. Depending on date the Jinty would be a Hasland or Westhouses engine. Would have been a fascinating place in the good old days.' ColourRail

First published in the United Kingdom in 2022,
by Irwell Press Limited, 59A, High Street, Clophill,
Bedfordshire MK45 4BE
Tel: 01525 861888
www.irwellpress.com

The JOY of JINTIES

The 3F 0-6-0Ts of the LMS and BR, 1924-1967

Part Two 47460-47579

Some Reminders from Part One

It's not necessary to repeat the entire Introductory Notes from Part One but the following outline comments might be useful. The true progenitors of the LMS Jinty were the sixty Johnson Midland 0-6-0Ts built over 1899-1902; all survived well into the 1950s and many into the 1960s. We'll see more of them in the final part.

It was this design, reboilered and altered/improved, that came to serve as the standard LMS shunting/trip engine, the 3F 'Jinty' which first appeared in 1924. On first sight the design was over twenty years old but although the Midland tanks dated from the turn of the century, they had been rebuilt from August 1919 (all were not done till 1942) with G5½ belpaire boilers and new cabs; they were in fact not only the engines most suited to the shunting/trip work of the new LMS but in their upgraded form were the most modern too, a design in effect only three years old. It was this 'upgraded' and thoroughly modern version that the LMS chose to replicate. Given the increasing need for such engines, the choice was between perpetuating a proven, suitable design of one of the constituent companies, or designing a new locomotive altogether. The design staff had other, more urgent fish to fry and, rightly, the Midland loco was deemed the best option. It was sturdy, reliable, used standard parts; it was economical and its role meant it was usually limited as to speed and distances worked, so the bearings were not overtaxed.

So it was that the provision of new '3F' 0-6-0Ts (they weren't called that then) was

simply waved through in 1923: 'Fifty 0-6-0 Shunting Tank Engines' along with numbers of 0-6-0s and 4-4-0s. They were to be built by outside contractors; twenty at Vulcan Foundry, fifteen by North British and fifteen at Hunslet.

All were in action by March 1925 but this was only the start, such was the need for an engine like this. Construction proceeded as indicated in this table (Rowledge, *Engines of the LMS 1923-1951*).

From 1928 the tanks got the power classification '3' then '3F' and mostly were referred to as '3F tank engines'. At some point the term 'Jocko' emerged among crews but this may have applied to any shunting type engine since ancient times. 'Dobbin', obviously derived from shunting horses was another term, common apparently in the East Midlands though it was also in use at Watford and probably elsewhere. No one can really say now how or when the

enthusiast name 'Jinty' came about. Or was it a 'enthusiast' term at all? Peter Groom recalls: *Even in 1952, presumably from reading Trains Illustrated, I 'knew' that railwaymen didn't call them Jinties, yet one of our group went to work at Leicester Midland shed and certainly found them to be called 'Jinties'. The Midland predecessors were 'Midland Jinties'!*

Lest the 3F tanks be remembered only as 'shunters' it can be noted that plenty of passenger work came their way at first, most famously the North London commuter workings out of Broad Street over the old GN.

A particular sphere of activity the Jinties made their own was the transfer freight. Such work abounded on the LMS and BR for years after that. Jinties were perfect for the role and doubtless this contributed greatly to their continued survival.

Original Nos.	1934 nos.	Lot	Year	Maker	Works No.
7100-7119	7260-7279	12	1924	Vulcan	3717-3736
7120-7134	7280-7294	13	1924	North British	23121-23135
7135-7141	7295-7301	14	1924	Hunslet	1460-1466
7142-7149	7302-7309	14	1925	Hunslet	1467-1674
7150-7156	*7310-7316*	ex-S&D, see below			
16400-16459	7317-7376	34	1926	North British	23396-23455
16460-16509	7377-7426	35	1926	Vulcan	3948-3997
16510-16518	7427-7435	36	1926	Hunslet	1511-1519
16519-16534	7436-7451	36	1927	Hunslet	1520-1535
16535-16543	7452-7560	37	1926	Bagnall	2288-2296
16544-16549	7461-7466	37	1927	Bagnall	2297-2302
16550-16554	7467-7471	50	1928	Vulcan	4175-4179
16555-16560	7472-7477	50	1927	Vulcan	4169-4174
16561-16599	7478-7516	50	1928	Vulcan	4180-4218
16600-16624	7517-7541	51	1928	Beardmore	325-349
16625-16632	7542-7549	52	1927	Hunslet	1558-1565
16633-16649	7550-7566	52	1928	Hunslet	1566-1582?
16650-16669	7567-7586	58	1928	Hunslet	1591-1610
16670-16674	7587-7591	58	1929	Hunslet	1611-1615
16675-16684	7592-7601	59	1928	Bagnall	2343-2352
16685-16723	7602-7640	60	1928	Beardmore	350-388
16724-16749	7641-7666	60	1929	Beardmore	389-414
16750-16764	7667-7681	82	1931	Horwich	-
Total 422					

7150-7156 were built by Bagnall for the Somerset & Dorset in 1928 where they bore the numbers 19-25. They were absorbed into LMS stock in 1930 to become 7150-7156 as above.

SOME DETAILS Edited and shortened from Part One

Safety Valves

The first fifty 7100-7149 (7260-7309) had the tall, elegant but somewhat archaic-looking Ramsbottom safety valves; the rest had Pop safety valves. Pop valves like the Ross version had helical springs in compression and occupied relatively little space. Pop valves allowed a much quicker release of pressure and the Ramsbottom valves began to go very much out of favour. The first fifty were converted to pop valves in fairly short order when a general change was made on the LMS from 1925.

Washout Plugs

Two were fitted either side on the firebox shoulders. There were others in the cab, lower down the firebox. There were covers, or 'doors' over the plugs except for the last fifteen built at Horwich in 1931 – these had simpler, more utilitarian plugs.

Lubrication

There was a single feed hydrostatic sight feed lubricator in the cab for valves and pistons. Everything else was by 'hand and wicks'. The prominent 3-feed delivery boxes on the tank fronts were for the axleboxes. Some later had 2-feed boxes because a Wakefield fountain lubricator was fitted. There were the little cup Furness lubricators for coasting on the early ones, either side of the smokebox saddle. Sight feeds only work when the regulator is open; the small Furness devices worked by feeding oil when the regulator was closed and the locos coasting. In 1928 it was concluded they served little good purpose; earlier engines had them removed and later ones did not have them. One or two did not have them finally removed till early BR days.

Brakes/Vacuum Ejector

The engines had the vacuum brake for train working and of course the steam brake for the engine itself. Exceptions were 16650-16749 (7567-7666) which had steam brakes only; because of the nature of the work they were expected to do they had three link instead of screw couplings but over the years plenty can be found with the latter. The characteristic piping and equipment attached to the hand rail (absent on the steam brake-only engines) on the right-hand side of the boiler between the smokebox and the tank combined 1 inch 'large' and ¾ inch 'small' ejector between the tank front and the smokebox.

Carriage Warming

A pool of 3F tanks capable of heating carriage stock was necessary because of their prominent role as station pilots, moving passenger stock and indeed early on as passenger engines on branches. There was even the London commuter work for a while.

The gear (permanent piping and hoses which were removed for maintenance in the summer) had been fitted to the first Midland engines back at the turn of the century and so too in turn were a number of the LMS engines; mostly it appeared new with the engines (sixty or more, including the seven S&D engines). Another fifty or so already in traffic were fitted in the 1920s and 1930s.

Cabs

A distinctive look to the engines was imparted by the way the cab was 'inset' with respect to the tanks. The curved roof had rainstrips but these were too high up and rain still dripped on a man looking out. New ones were welded in over a number of years. There was a prominent ventilator on the roof which could be raised and angled front or aft; it often became jammed as the years stretched on between overhauls.

Sanding

There was steam sanding to the front and rear of the middle driving wheels with boxes below the running plate either side. The front one was conventional enough, with a filler above on the running plate but the filler for the rear one was on top of the side tank, with a pipe running

Continues page 10.

47461 fresh from works attention, at Derby MPD on 11 July 1958. Repairs to the tank and bunker sheets (a severe 'sideswipe' by the look of it) appear to have been put in the hands of a junior apprentice. It is on its way home to Rowsley, recently recoded 17C as per the newly painted shed plate. R.J. Buckley, Initial Photographics.

47460

Built as 16543 at Bagnall, Stafford December 1926
Works no.2296
Renumbered 7460 23/1/36; 47460 w/e 23/4/49
3/11/39 Manually operated blowdown valve
23/4/49 Fitting independent steam brake valves
Withdrawn w/e 18/5/63

47460 Repairs	
24/7/29-7/8/29LS	44,040
18/1/31-12/2/31HG	28,237
4/3/34-21/3/34LS	63,829
16/12/35-23/1/36HG	39,477
19/2/37-15/4/37LO	27,091
3/4/39-10/10/39LS	51,158
22/2/40-2/3/40LO	9,383
14/5/41-7/6/41HG	33,461
7/12/43-4/1/44LS	64,614
15/3/46-13/4/46HG	52,786
30/3/49-21/4/49LI	80,256 Derby
12/4/52-9/5/52HG	80,912 Derby
11/4/55-26/4/55HI	75,340 Derby
12/4/58-30/4/58HG	67,097 Derby
13/11/61-30/11/61LI	87,391 Derby

47460 Sheds	
Buxton	1/1/27
Rowsley	28/9/35

47460 Boilers	
No.6789	7/6/41
No.7853	13/4/46
No.6873	9/5/52
No.10524	30/4/58

47461

Built as 16544 at Bagnall, Stafford 29th April 1927
Works no.2297
Renumbered 7461 21/6/35; 47461 w/e 8/10/49
1/6/32 Clips for coal slackingpipe
28/6/37 Fitting protection plates for vacuum stand pipes
28/6/37 Fitting Independent steam brake valves
28/6/37 Fitting continuous blowdown apparatus
Withdrawn w/e 12/9/64

47461 Repairs	
5/10/29-24/10/29LS	46,822
21/7/31-31/7/31LS	52,629
12/5/32-1/6/32HG	19,451
16/1/34-3/2/34LO	34,139
31/5/35-21/6/35HS	31,608
3/6/37-28/6/37HG	49,265
20/9/39-30/9/39LS	58,602
12/11/41-9/12/41HG	116,108
27/5/44-17/6/44HS	66,693
11/2/47-7/3/47HG	59,828 Derby
11/9/49-6/10/49HI	71,525 Derby
22/11/52-15/12/52HI	82,220 Derby
9/8/55-26/8/55LI	67,399 Derby
6/6/58-27/6/58HG	66,897 Derby
29/1/62-22/2/62HG	- Derby

47461 Sheds	
Buxton	26/10/27
Rowsley	28/9/35
Derby	2/5/64
Birkenhead	9/8/64
Derby	31/8/64

47461 Boilers	
No.10026	15/6/37
No.11084	9/12/41
No.6854	7/3/47
No.7888	15/12/52
No.10235	27/6/58

47462

Built as 16545 at Bagnall, Stafford 8th April 1927
Works no.2298
Renumbered 7462 3/2/37; 47462 w/e 11/2/50
23/1/32 Clips for coal slacking pipe
1/12/35 Regulator handle extension
5/2/37 Fitting protection plates for vacuum stand pipes
5/2/37 Fitting light shield for sliding fire doors
5/2/37 Fitting independent steam brake valves
5/2/37 Fitting continuous blowdown apparatus
Withdrawn w/e 30/9/61

47462 Repairs	
4/11/29-21/11/29LS	53,165
5/1/32-23/1/32HG	40,124
21/3/35-26/3/35LO	72,497
21/6/35-19/7/35LS	5,284
16/1/36-24/1/36LO	18,140
25/6/36-2/7/36LO	10,452
18/1/37-5/2/37HG	12,750
14/2/38-21/2/38LO	26,007
14/2/40-28/3/40HS	49,851
10/3/42-18/3/42LO	58,923
5/12/42-13/1/43LS	14,723
25/3/44-30/3/44LO	36,194
24/1/45-19/2/45HG	21,554
8/9/47-17/10/47LS	70,044 Leeds
9/1/50-6/2/50HG	55,560 Derby
7/1/53-26/1/53HI	75,859 Derby
24/1/56-9/2/56HG	68,470 Derby

47462 Sheds	
Gloucester	26/10/27
Bradford	22/3/30
Leeds	11/7/31
Royston	28/9/35
Starbeck	17/11/57
York	13/9/59
Goole	4/10/59
Stored serviceable	
13/9/59-4/10/59	
18/12/60-22/9/61	

47462 Boilers	
No.7541	28/3/40
No.6861	19/2/45
No.10525	6/2/50
No.14133	9/2/56

47463

Built as 16546 at Bagnall, Stafford April 1927
Works no.2299
Renumbered 7463 16/11/36; 47463 w/e 10/9/49
16/11/36 Removal of injector overflow gear
6/9/41 Manually operated blowdown valve
4/10/41 Fitting steel in lieu of copper boiler tubes
10/9/49 Modifications to trailing sand boxes
10/9/49 Fitting independent steam brake valve
Withdrawn w/e 3/12/60

47463 Repairs	
11/11/29-3/12/29LS	51,788
29/9/30-7/10/30LO	14,640
28/4/31-12/5/31LO	13,749
5/8/31-3/9/31HG	4,725
26/11/32-30/12/32LO	?
20/6/32-4/7/32LO	17,824
2/10/33-17/10/33LO	40,112
17/3/34-14/4/34LO	51,113
23/8/35-7/9/35LS	30,005
27/7/36-16/11/36HG	23,987
30/10/39-17/11/39LS	75,398
21/7/41-15/8/41HG	44,569
7/2/44-22/3/44LS	75,951
25/11/46-21/12/46HG	71,106 Derby
24/8/49-6/9/49HI	78,042 Derby
7/2/53-6/3/53HG	66,828 Derby
14/5/56-24/5/56LI	61,910 Derby
21/6/57-31/7/57HG	23,000 Derby

47463 Sheds	
Gloucester	26/10/27
Leeds	17/5/30
Normanton	11/7/31
Stourton	16/3/35
Ardsley	18/5/58
Wakefield	22/2/59
Mirfield	25/9/60

47463 Boilers	
No.6785	15/8/41
No.8091	21/12/46
No.14036	6/3/53
No.13645	31/7/57

47462, date/location unrecorded. Its last Heavy General predated the provision of the second emblem and this Jinty kept the original one to the end. This is quite possibly Crewe, where the engine was sent to meet its maker in 1961. Rail Archive Stephenson.

A Jinty posed for the official record for once – shaded numbers and lettering on 7463, renumbered from 16546 in 1936. The new front number plate has the 'block' pattern. The filler lid moved from the 'keyhole' to the top of the sand box is visible. Rail Archive Stephenson.

16547 (7464, 47464) possibly at Holbeck, in the days before renumbering to 7464. Rail Archive Stephenson.

47464 in the Burton roundhouse in the early 1960s, together with long-term Burton cohabitant, 47643. RailOnline

47464

Built as 16547 at Bagnall, Stafford 22nd May 1927
Works no.2300
Renumbered 7464 7/6/37; 47464 w/e 27/8/49
7/6/37 Contiuous blowdown valves
22/1/44 Fitting steel instead of copper boiler tubes
27/12/52 Fitting independent steam brake valves
Withdrawn w/e 25/9/65

47464 Repairs	
23/10/29-8/11/29LO	50,506
11/12/29-20/12/29LS	2,581
29/10/31-13/11/31LO	33,331
24/4/32-12/5/32HG	9,929
26/5/33-22/6/33LO	20,157
6/9/34-13/9/34LO	27,508
6/11/35-3/11/35LS	22,682
24/4/37-7/6/37HG	23,825
24/9/41-18/10/41LS	74,832
16/1/42-17/2/42LO	3,378
10/12/43-14/1/44HG	55,592
27/8/46-27/9/46HS	70,704
7/7/49-23/8/49HG	63,806 Derby
10/11/52-4/12/52LI	85,650 Derby
7/11/55-1/12/55HG	79,825 Derby
25/11/58-23/12/58LI	82,522 Derby
28/11/61-22/12/61HG	- Derby

47464 Sheds	
Gloucester	26/10/27
Normanton	11/7/31
Carlton	16/3/35
Widnes	23/3/35
Burton	20/12/41
Mold Jct	31/8/46
Burton	14/9/46
Bromsgrove	30/11/57
Burton	28/12/57
Stored serviceable 21/6/65-25/9/65	

47464 Boilers	
No.5485	1/6/37
No.11879	14/1/44
No.11670	23/8/49
No.13305	1/12/55

47465

Built as 16548 at Bagnall, Stafford 19th June 1927
Works no.2301
Renumbered 7465 27/3/35; 47465 w/e 10/9/49
8/10/32 Fitting Menno grease cups
4/2/37 Independent steam brake valves
26/11/38 Manually operated blowdown valves
Withdrawn w/e 15/6/63

47465 Repairs	
10/1/30-31/1/30LS	53,011
3/8/31-28/8/31HG	80,215
14/9/34-3/10/34LS	71,334
31/1/35-29/3/35HO	80,116
8/1/37-4/2/37HS	45,594
15/2/40-1/3/40HG	70,402
28/12/42-13/1/43LO	60,264
25/5/44-9/6/44HS	77,335
7/10/48-19/10/48LO	56,138 Shed
16/8/49-7/9/49HG	63,471 Derby
21/3/52-28/4/52HI	31,212 Derby
26/3/56-17/4/56HG	53,509 Derby

47465 Sheds	
Gloucester	26/10/27
Radstock	21/3/42

47465 Boilers	
No.7812	1/3/40
No.5480	9/6/44
No.7555	7/9/49
No.10525	17/4/56

Bromsgrove's 47465 at Bath Green Park in 1955; it was a harsh winter (note the brazier to protect the water column from freezing) though a heat wave followed in August – this is Britain after all and nothing changes. 47465 has been appropriated for snowplough duties and will be/would have been on call for a while. It has ploughs fore and aft with all buffers removed.
RailOnline

How a lined Jinty might have looked! Bagnall did up its 16549 (7466, 47466) in an imagined lining in order to record it photographically in 1927. Note the eccentric top front lamp iron. Temporary liveries like this were often employed by manufacturers and the railways themselves (the famous 'photographic grey') to bring out as much detail as possible for record/publicity purposes. 16549 was delivered in plain black, be assured!

several feet down through to the box all that way below under the running plate. As well as the inconvenience of a ladder, or clambering up from the front, the pipe (it ran through the water space) might leak with unfortunate effects on the sanding. After the first fifty the well-known cut-out at the base of the tanks was made to accommodate a filler lid at a more convenient position atop the running plate. This too for some reason was not found satisfactory and over the years from the 1940s to the middle 1950s the filler lid was moved to the rear sand box itself, where it sat largely invisible to the outside world. The cut-out famously remained, giving rise to the 'clockwork key' jibe. The first fifty engines were never altered so never bore the famous cut-out.

Bunkers
It might be thought that a big solid feature like a bunker might be timeless; unchanged and unchanging but no... The original Midland engines had bunkers that were flat – vertical – at the rear but the LMS ones had a rearward curved extension increasing the capacity to 2½ tons. It was topped by a pair of coal rails, fairly rudimentary-looking and reminiscent of a crude grate. A familiar addition came in the form of

a hinged plate on the rear part. Its purpose was apparently to inhibit spillage at coaling plants though it also enabled a few extra lumps to be put on board. Coal falling down while under mechanical plants in particular could also damage the vacuum pipes below so a small plate, looking like a footstep, was fitted above the pipe, to shield it. On a few locos six of the grate-like rails appeared instead of the original two and one or two engines found themselves with three or four such rails.

ATC
A few Jinties associated with the London Tilbury & Southend system got the native Hudd Automatic Train Control (ATC) brought into use in the mid-1930s. A number of engines on that line were overhauled at Bow Works but the bigger ones, the passenger tanks, went to and from two works for overhaul – once to Bow for removal of the Hudd gear before going off to (usually) Derby and then again to Bow on their return for the gear to be re-fitted. A Jinty more often would go to Bow only but some too, if going to Derby, went through the 'before and after' Bow process.

In the event of an engine transferring off the 'Tilbury' a quick visit to Bow was necessary for removal of its Hudd gear, for it was

no use in Warrington, or Swansea. Transfer to Willesden or Watford though (see 47307 at Watford for instance) would see the gear kept on just in case, it seems. The record cards, as usual, are less than explicit but there are a few entries 'Fitting ATC gear'. Dozens of 3F tanks – the waters are muddied by the Devons Road Bow allocation – went to and from the LT&S in the years after the Hudd system was instigated but whether it was fitted to all of them is hard to say.

Pull/Push
Vacuum Controlled Regulators (VCR) for pull/push, or motor working, had been fitted to Midland 0-6-0Ts and then transferred to 0-4-4Ts before the Great War. The gear had been removed by 1919. VCRs were revived when LMS 3F tanks 16560-16564 (7477-7481 – see pictures in later volume) were so equipped in 1934 for motor trains in South Wales; the engines were stationed at Upper Bank and worked out of Swansea St Thomas and Victoria stations. The external manifestation of the push/pull gear was a cylinder and rodding on the left-hand side of the smokebox, with vacuum created by the existing ejectors.

Continues page 13.

47466

Built as 16549 at Bagnall, Stafford 19th June 1927
Works no.2302
Renumbered 7466 20/1/38; 47466 w/e 15/4/50
8/7/38 Manually operated blowdown valves
8/7/38 Independent steam brake valves
30/11/57 Modified pistons for continuous blowdown valves
Withdrawn w/e 8/9/62

47466 Repairs	
26/2/30-14/3/30LS	44,858
8/3/31-9/4/31HG	13,847
4/1/32-19/1/32LO	10,977
29/3/34-18/5/34LS	54,555
30/10/35-14/1/36HG	34,143
2/6/38-8/7/38HS	57,783
18/6/40-6/7/40LS	54,692
21/3/42-24/4/42HG	55,841
22/12/43-15/1/44LS	57,727
9/8/45-29/9/45HS	53,630
25/9/47-29/10/47HG	65,288 Derby
27/3/50-13/4/50LI	77,714 Derby
7/5/52-16/6/52HG	63,812 Derby
29/11/54-15/12/54LI	71,143 Derby
11/11/57-29/11/57HG	83,436 Derby

47466 Sheds	
Gloucester	26/10/27
Bristol	1/1/29
Nottingham	16/4/32
Birmingham	30/10/33
Saltley	28/9/35
Nottingham	14/1/36
Westhouses	22/10/38

47466 Boilers	
No.7499	24/4/42
No.10026	29/10/47
No.7853	16/6/52
No.10022	29/11/57

47467

Built as 16550 at the Vulcan Foundry 4th January 1928
Works No.4175
Renumbered 7467 27/11/37; 47467 w/e 26/2/49
22/11/37 Manually operated blowdown valves
26/2/49 Fitting steel in lieu of copper boiler tubes
26/2/49 Fitting independent steam brake valves
26/2/49 Modification to trailing sand boxes
Withdrawn w/e 26/9/64

47467 Repairs	
9/4/30-10/5/30LO	48,073
8/1/31-30/1/31LS	17,968
4/12/32-22/1/32HS	38,644
10/9/35-28/9/35HG	68,108
4/11/37-22/11/37HG	51,820
23/7/40-13/8/40HS	67,838
20/3/43-10/4/43HG	63,369
Damaged by enemy action 24/2/44 Euston	
4/3/46-13/4/46LS	41,648
14/1/49-24/2/49HG	26,988 Derby
7/5/53-1/6/53HI	45,138 Derby
1/3/54-2/4/54HG	8,412 Derby
25/5/60-7/7/60HG	85,807 Derby

47467 Sheds	
Warrington	4/1/28
Derby	14/1/28
Devons Road	26/9/28
Camden	25/9/29
Crewe South	14/6/58

47467 Boilers	
No.6804	15/11/37
No.6833	10/4/43
No.6874	24/2/49
No.14055	2/4/54
No.11557	7/7/60

47467 at Crewe South in the 1960s. To the left on its way to the works (or on its way back) is Tyne Dock 2-10-0 92061.
RailOnline

47468

Built as 16551 at the Vulcan Foundry Ltd. 5th January 1928
Works No.4176
Renumbered 7468 11/6/37; 47468 w/e 8/4/50
23/4/50 Fitting independent steam brake valves
Withdrawn w/e 23/1/65

47468 Repairs	
24/8/30-13/9/30LS	44,984
26/8/31-16/9/31HG	20,869
17/1/34-8/2/34HS	59,928
4/4/35-4/5/35LS	33,489
26/5/37-11/6/37HS	52,026
1/2/39-7/10/39HG	44,700
24/2/42-11/3/42LS	73,544
7/10/43-1/12/43HG	44,734
21/3/47-10/4/47LO	101,896 Shed
29/7/47-22/8/47HS	8,025 Derby
3/3/50-4/4/50HG	70,631 Derby
29/12/52-21/1/53LI	71,320 Derby
17/9/54-15/10/54HG	46,352 Derby
8/5/57-29/5/57HG	70,375 Derby
12/9/60-1/12/60HG	84,982 Derby

47468 Sheds	
Bradford	1/29
Lancaster	12/29
Carnforth	8/8/64
Rose Grove	3/10/64
Fleetwood	31/10/64

47468 Boilers	
No.7837	7/10/39
No.5487	1/12/43
No.6843	4/4/50
No.10240	15/10/54
No.13973	29/5/57
No.14311	1/12/60

47469

Built as 16552 at The Vulcan Foundry Ltd. 6th January 1928
Works No.4177
Renumbered 7469 30/5/35; 47469 w/e 11/11/50
26/12/31 Clips for coal slacking pipe
3/6/35 Experimental trial of 'Houghltokote' heat resisting pipe
14/7/35 Trial of asbestos fibre for packing gauge frames
26/11/38 Manually operated blowdown valves
15/5/43 Fitting steel in lieu of copper boiler tubes
2/12/50 Fitting independent steam brake valves
Withdrawn w/e 11/1/64

47469 Repairs	
21/8/30-12/9/30LS	57,307
6/3/31-2/4/31LO	10,295
2/12/31-19/12/31HG	14,453
28/12/33-10/1/34LS	49,601
13/5/35-3/6/35HG	32,086
18/3/37-17/4/37HO	49,192
22/6/38-7/7/38LS	32,271
19/6/40-3/7/40HG	54,413
22/3/43-23/4/43HS	81,480
23/4/46-16/5/46HG	92,777
13/2/48-3/4/48LS	50,221 Leeds
30/8/50-10/11/50HG	66,694 Derby
2/12/53-31/12/53HI	84,655 Derby
11/9/56-3/10/56HG	69,432 Derby
8/1/60-19/2/60HG	93,846 Derby

47469 Shed	
Lancaster	1/1929

47469 Boilers	
No.6876	3/7/40
No.6856	16/5/46
No.13634	10/11/50
No.11552	3/10/56
No.14381	19/2/60

Lancaster's 47468 at Heysham Harbour on 4 September 1962. The two main pilot turns here, the North Side and South Side shunts, were the province of Lancaster Green Ayre MPD. The sheer complexity of it all, and the vast quantity of it, is now largely forgotten with respect to freight working on the steam age railway. In this one ordinary corner of the kingdom, shunts and trips went on endlessly, much of it in time-honoured fashion between the 'Midland' and the 'LNW' side. One of the first and certainly one of the best 'steam autobiographies' is *London Midland Fireman* by Mike Higson (Ian Allan, 1972) and in it he details much of the work here, in an entertaining style. RailOnline

The Joy of a Jinty (complete with coal on roof). A sparkling 47470 with 'space reserved' for the emblem, at Derby after a Heavy General, August 1948. Rail Archive Stephenson.

Footsteps

As any Engine Picker knows, if a component, part or feature can be altered, it probably will be. The likelihood of difference will probably be inversely proportional to its importance in the overall design but it will nevertheless be reasoned and practical. Take footsteps. The 'step' part was flat but boots could slip off with nasty results so they were turned up at the corners in the interests of safety. The earlier 'flat' ones were all altered accordingly, in the 1930s.

Buffers

On most long-lived classes buffers evolved to a more robust form. Even buffers wore out and the Midland style ones, which had packing plates behind (buffers on the original MR engines had two or three such plates, sometimes made in wood) gave way to more modern buffers with tread plates on top of the body.

Livery

Black, passing fairly rapidly to grimy grey, draped in scale, was more often than not the lot of the Jinty. Nevertheless, variations in lettering, numbering and so on, abounded... The usual dictum applies – if you

really do want a model to represent a particular narrowly defined period, then you need photographs. Validating the date scribbled on the back of the photograph is another thing...

The curious vermillion rectangles ('panels') with LMS appeared on 7100-7149 of 1924-25 and the first fifty or so in the series from 16400 of 1926 but given the somewhat erratic cleaning regime enjoyed by the Jinties these little panels, never prominent in the best of circumstances, must have rapidly disappeared, fading from view under the grime. It was almost irrelevant that the style of the panel was altered halfway through from concave to conventionally rounded – convex I suppose you'd say in this context – corners. Numbers were lovely and large, in serif, on the tank sides. These were 14 inches high though some individuals later got 18 inch high letters which appeared truly enormous.

From the late 1920s engine numbers (10 inches for reasons of space) were on the bunker sides with 14 inch L M S on the tanks, a more logical

arrangement. Several variations, normally ascribed to human error, occurred before the War. Introduced in that decade – complicating matters – was a quite fetching almost art deco shaded block pattern. Unfortunately this was extended to no more than three engines - *LMS Locomotive Profiles No.14* (see acknowledgement below) is exhaustive on this sort of thing, as it is on all aspects of the Jinties it must be said.

Renumbering from the 16XXX series in the 1930s and then the addition of 40,000 under BR made for further variations of course. The sublime 1946 livery was not applied to any humble 3F tank.

Nationalisation was most notable early on for the BRITISH RAILWAYS in full in various sizes, styles and spacings while 47569 got the first emblem between the BRITISH and the RAILWAYS. Plenty had the gap between the two words to take the emblem but never got it. A couple got the rather pointless 'M' prefix.

47470

Built as 16553 at The Vulcan Foundry Ltd. 10th January 1928
Works No.4178
Renumbered 7470 24/5/34; 47470 w/e 21/8/48
24/3/51 Fitting independent steam brake valves
Withdrawn w/e 23/6/62

47470 Repairs	
22/7/30-14/8/30LS	53,448
20/12/30-15/1/31LO	7,578
1/5/32-19/5/32HG	25,665
12/3/34-24/5/34HS	48,366
23/10/35-2/12/35HS	35,543
27/10/37-12/11/37LS	55,101
29/9/38-13/12/38HG	24,745
20/4/40-1/6/40HS	35,173
13/2/43-16/3/43HG	68,347
12/3/45-21/4/45LS	67,149
1/7/48-20/8/48HG	79,790 Derby
22/1/51-28/2/51LI	73,163 Derby
26/8/54-23/9/54HG	96,999 Derby
7/7/58-8/8/58HI	99,107 Derby
26/4/60-17/6/60HG	47,543 Derby

47470 Shed	
Lancaster	1/1929

47470 Boilers	
No.7832	13/12/38
No.5478	16/3/43
No.11085	20/8/48
No.13990	23/9/54
No.14102	17/6/60

47471

Built as 16554 at The Vulcan Foundry Ltd. 11th January 1928
Works No.4179
Renumbered 7471 24/1/36; 47471 w/e 4/6/49
20/1/38 Manually operated blowdown valves
19/2/44 Fitting steel in lieu of copper boiler tubes
18/6/49 Fitting independent steam brake valves
18/6/49 Modifications to trailing sand boxes
Withdrawn w/e 31/12/66

47471 Repairs	
2/5/30-31/5/30LS	58,468
22/4/31-5/6/31LO	18,115
27/10/31-10/11/31LS	9,459
13/1/33-9/2/33HG	23,476
13/1/36-29/1/36LS	60,859
6/1/38-20/1/38HG	45,674
25/9/40-16/10/40LS	72,312
7/8/42-4/9/42HS	53,155
6/1/44-5/2/44HG	39,829
3/10/46-24/10/46HS	79,683 Derby
2/5/49-2/6/49HG	71,857 Derby
4/6/52-18/6/52LI	84,800 Derby
14/1/55-8/2/55HG	70,028 Derby
27/8/58-12/9/58LI	97,486 Derby
2/10/59-9/11/59HC	26,315 Derby
19/11/59-9/11/59NC(rect)	53 Derby
10/2/63-25/1/63HI	- Derby

47471 Sheds	
Lancaster	1/1929
Nottingham	4/11/33
Lancaster	14/3/36
Carnforth	18/6/60
Kingmoor	17/9/60

47471 Boilers	
No.6837	12/1/38
No.7516	5/2/44
No.7566	2/6/49
No.14121	8/2/55
No.14384	9/11/59

47470 ex-works (one not involving a repaint obviously) at Derby shed on 30 August 1958; the engine only ever worked from Lancaster Green Ayre. How one engine stayed at a single shed its entire life while others had a dozen or more moves is one those eternal mysteries of engine-picking. Peter Groom.

Above. 47471 thoroughly begrimed (the emblem having disappeared) in the 1960s. The location is almost certainly Kingmoor, if I've identified the building in the background correctly as the breakdown crane shed. Rail Archive Stephenson.

Middle. 47472 came to Lostock Hall in 1961 and until its withdrawal five years later could very often be found piloting at the station, its smokebox door straps whitened to mark its work in the public eye. At some time in that period, it has a few carriages, to be attached or recently detached from a train. RailOnline

Bottom. The reason for 47472's longevity and why other Jinties lasted till 1966 and beyond was a late Heavy General coming to the rescue. So for all the criticism of short-lived engines, the last (overhauled) Jinties in the main faithfully eked out their days. Here is 47472 at Derby MPD (turntable to the right) after a final Heavy General, in November 1961.

47472 at home at Lostock Hall MPD in September 1965 during bouts as Preston station pilot. At this time it was noted as often sharing the duty with 47293. A feature pointed out frequently in these volumes are the representative electrification masts and wires, erected at most sheds to acquaint crews with the dangerous proximity of the OHL (Overhead Line). RailOnline

47472, still at its Lostock Hall home, on 29 May 1966, a few months before withdrawal. RailOnline

47472

Built as 16555 at The Vulcan Foundry Ltd. 31st December 1927
Works No.4169
Renumbered 7472 29/7/35; 47472 w/e 2/7/49
31/1/38 Independent steam brake valves
31/3/38 Manually operated blowdown valves
15/5/43 Regulator handle extension
15/5/43 Fitting steel in lieu of copper boiler tubes
16/7/49 Modifications to trailing sand boxes
10/8/57 Modified pistons for continuous blowdown valves
Withdrawn w/e 26/11/66

47472 Repairs		
5/8/30-13/8/30LS	68,960	
28/11/32-8/12/32HG	46,081	
26/6/35-29/7/35HS	56,039	
26/5/37-29/6/37LO	45,447	
18/1/38-31/1/38HG	13,584	
25/7/40-3/8/40LS	74,796	
1/2/41-15/2/41LO	13,587	
9/2/42-21/2/42HS	14,712	
11/1/43-29/1/43LO	14,843	
6/4/43-28/4/43HG	5,103	
26/2/46-21/3/46HS	55,644	
19/8/47-26/9/47LO	26,935	Derby
31/5/49-29/6/49HG	61,781	Derby
16/5/51-21/6/51HI	35,599	Derby
12/1/54-3/2/54HG	53.044	Derby
2/7/57-5/8/57HG	103,234	Derby
18/9/61-24/11/61HG	124,057	Derby
21/6/63-5/7/63LC	-	Horwich

47472 Sheds	
Warrington	24/12/27
Birkenhead	31/12/27
Stoke	19/5/28
Holyhead	25/1/36
Speke Jct	1/6/40
Birkenhead	24/11/45
Stoke	24/5/52
Preston	15/8/53
Lostock Hall	16/9/61

47472 Boilers	
No.7474	24/1/38
No.6845	28/4/43
No.10025	29/6/49
No.6744	3/2/54
No.13991	5/8/57
No.14113	24/11/61

47473

Built as 16556 at The Vulcan Foundry Ltd. 31st December 1927
Works No.4170
Renumbered 7473 15/4/35; 47473 w/e 16/10/48
11/6/38 Manually operated blowdown valves
2/10/43 Fitting steel in lieu of copper boiler tubes
27/2/54 Fitting independent steam brake valves
Withdrawn w/e 17/2/62

47473 Repairs		
20/6/30-28/7/30LS	60,237	
11/9/32-28/9/32LS	41,839	
10/7/33-19/7/33HG	16,764	
9/4/35-15/4/35LS	42,211	
14/4/37-4/5/37LS	30,434	
25/10/38-15/12/38HG	37,197	
27/2/41-17/3/41LS	61,947	
15/9/43-28/9/43HG	64,158	
17/7/46-3/8/46LO	69,147	
20/9/46-21/10/46HS	3.014	
15/9/48-13/10/48HG	45,856	Bow
8/1/51-26/1/51HG	71,362	Derby
1/1/54-4/2/54LI	91,231	Derby
23/2/54-25/2/54NC(rect)	475	Bow
13/3/54-25/3/54LC	1,289	Bow
14/1/56-3/2/56HG	40,718	Derby
25/11/58-19/12/58LI	58,793	Bow

47473 Sheds	
Warrington	24/12/27
Stoke	7/1/28
Bushbury	16/11/35
Carnforth	5/11/60

47473 Boilers	
No.7508	15/12/38
No.6825	28/9/43
No.7337	13/10/48
No.6761	26/1/51
No.14134	3/2/56

47473 at Bushbury MPD late in 1949, maybe 1950; the Wolverhampton shed had been its home since 1935 and it did not leave till 1960. The whitewash will be a leftover of the Blackout. Look closely and a remarkable feature of this Jinty is revealed, a thin (red) lining on the tanks (it extended to the bunker sides, cab and running valence too). *LMS Locomotive Profiles* (see acknowledgements) muses that it was applied during repairs at Rugby shops, presumably during a rush of blood to the head. BRITISH RAILWAYS is in 6 inch with space for the emblem and the number in 8 inch. In 1949 the engine was notable for carrying the chalked notice on the smokebox door WOLVES 3 LEICESTER 1 which was indeed the result of the 1949 Cup Final, and not a prediction. RailOnline

47474

Built as 16557 at The Vulcan Foundry Ltd 31st December 1927
Works No.4171
Renumbered 7474 17/1/36; 47474 w/e 21/1/50
21/2/38 Manually operated blowdown valves
21/2/38 Independent steam brake valves
2/1/44 Fitting steel in lieu of copper boiler tubes
Withdrawn w/e 1/9/62

47474 Repairs	
16/6/30-18/7/30LS	59,040
4/2/33-15/2/33HG	51,080
18/7/34-24/7/34LO	35,202
8/1/36-17/1/36LS	30,398
6/4/36-28/4/36LO	5,956
8/2/38-21/2/38HG	39,046
26/12/40-9/1/41LS	64,509
8/1/44-20/1/44HG	59,568
6/2/47-15/3/47HS	56,841 Derby
23/12/49-17/1/50HG	53,229 Bow
10/6/53-1/7/53LI	67,873 Bow
6/11/56-7/12/56HG	51,408 Bow

47474 Sheds	
Warrington	24/12/27
Stoke	7/1/28
Longsight	19/10/35
Rugby	7/12/35
Willesden	29/9/45
Monument Lane	26/10/57
Aston	10/2/62
Stafford	3/3/62

47474 Boilers	
No.6672	11/2/38
No.11874	20/1/44
No.13319	17/1/50
No.6745	7/12/56

47475

Built as 16558 at The Vulcan Foundry Ltd 31st December 1927
Works No.4172
Renumbered 7475 6/9/34; 47475 w/e 17/9/49
26/2/37 Continuous blowdown gear
2/6/37 Independent steam brake valves
2/6/37 Removal of injector overflow gear
Withdrawn w/e 24/2/62

47475 Repairs	
18/8/30-5/9/30LS	64,691
8/11/32-22/11/32HS	44,361
27/8/34-6/9/34LS	38,396
9/1/37-26/2/37HG	53,532
24/4/39-10/5/39LO	48,531
3/2/40-6/3/40LS	17,823
24/6/41-23/7/41LO	33,285
13/2/43-27/2/43HG	31,782
5/2/47-8/3/47LS	80,221 Bow
27/6/49-14/9/49HG	40,778 Bow
22/1/53-20/2/53LI	70,122 Bow
13/1/56-23/2/56HG	46,188 Bow

47475 Sheds	
Warrington	24/12/27
Stoke	7/1/28
Patricroft	11/4/36
Willesden	1/3/41
Kingmoor	15/3/58
Stafford	17/1/59

47475 Boilers	
No.7502	26/2/37
No.7878	27/2/43
No.7485	14/9/49
No.13324	23/2/56

47476

Built as 16559 at the Vulcan Foundry Ltd. 31st December 1927
Works No.4173
Renumbered 7476 11/1/35; 47476 w/e 13/8/49
26/11/37 Manually operated blowdown valves
26/11/37 Independent steam brake valves
26/11/37 Removal of injectors overflow gear
21/2/42 Fitting steel in lieu of copper boiler tubes
21/2/42 Regulator handle extension
Withdrawn w/e 9/5/64

47476 Repairs	
20/5/30-1/7/30HS	58,926
29/6/31-20/7/31LS	24,675
28/3/33-24/4/33HG	58,084
31/12/34-11/1/35HS	35,880
28/10/37-26/11/37HS	48,383
27/4/40-8/5/40LS	28,891
15/1/42-14/2/42HG	59,840
28/4/44-16/5/44HS	52,353
5/2/46-21/2/46HS	41,784
18/6/49-9/8/49LI	97,538 Derby
20/9/51-14/11/51HG	59,088 Derby
17/3/54-1/4/54LI	65,102 Derby
25/4/57-31/5/57HG	78,305 Derby
19/6/61-29/6/61HI	97,683

47476 Sheds	
Warrington	24/12/27
Stoke	7/1/28
Warrington	2/11/35
Springs Branch	11/1/36
Warrington	31/10/42
Holyhead	21/7/45
Stored serviceable 27/1/63-9/5/64	

47476 Boilers	
No.5821	17/11/37
No.11137	14/2/42
No.7818	21/2/46
No.13971	14/11/51
No.13964	31/5/57

Looking all action despite being stationary, 7474 works the coaling line under the giant plant at Willesden MPD, probably about 1949; carriage shed behind. You wouldn't want it appearing as a Euston pilot looking like this... Rail Archive Stephenson.

Fellow Willesden Jinty at more or less the same time; a near enough mirror image of 7474. Rail Archive Stephenson.

47476 shunting a postal train – one of the Irish Mails no less – late in the 1950s; the engine was long at Holyhead and this is surely the location. My understanding is that some Travelling Post Offices (TPOs) at least required turning on arrival – at Penzance for instance. This meant taking the stock to the Chacewater triangle, if I read my *Pre-Grouping Gazetteer* aright, which was some miles off. Apparently the Irish Mails only picked up in the down direction so the train didn't require turning. Post from Ireland presumably was loaded from trolleys and further sorted in London.

Life and Times of 47479 1. Early years at Devons Road as 16562; POTTERS BAR board for working the GN. Rail Archive Stephenson.

47477

Built as 16560 at The Vulcan Foundry Ltd. 31st December 1927
Works No.4174
Renumbered 7477 13/8/36; 47477 w/e 6/8/49
5/4/34 Vacuum control gear
13/8/36 Fitting of independent steam brake valves
13/8/36 Removal of Injector overflow gear
13/6/42 Continuous blowdown gear
13/6/42 Regulator handle extension
13/6/42 Fitting steel in lieu of copper boiler tubes
Withdrawn w/e 19/12/59

47477 Repairs	
4/7/30-4/8/30HS	64,011
16/11/32-24/11/32LS	48,971
14/3/34-5/4/34HG	33,856
29/7/36-13/8/36HS	64,914
18/9/38-20/10/38HG	62,879
16/10/40-12/11/40HS	59,600
30/4/42-28/5/42HG	42,786
20/9/44-4/10/44LS	59,200
6/8/46-24/8/46HG	38,942
23/10/47-26/11/47LO	31,615 Derby
4/7/49-5/8/49HG	30,916 Derby
4/1/50-26/1/50LC	10,233 Derby
2/7/52-6/8/52LI	59,927 Derby
14/8/52-19/8/52NC(rect)	367 Derby
26/2/55-16/3/55HG	47,152 Derby

47477 Sheds	
Warrington	31/12/27
Stoke	7/1/28
Longsight	15/10/30
Swansea	25/11/31
Upper Bank	28/10/33
Bank Hall	9/11/57
Stored Unserviceable 21/2/59-19/12/59	

47477 Boilers	
No.6744	20/10/38
No.5551	28/5/42
No.6876	24/8/46
No.6784	5/8/49
No.7529	16/3/55

47478

Built as 16561 at The Vulcan Foundry Ltd. 12th January 1928
Works No.4180
Renumbered 7478 17/4/34; 47478 w/e 23/10/48
17/4/34 Vacuum control gear
30/1/36 Trial of cast iron piston rod packing
30/1/36 Fitting cup leather type of piston packing
26/7/37 Manually operated blowdown valves
26/7/37 Removal of injectors overflow gear
13/5/44 Fitting steel in lieu of copper boiler tubes
27/11/48 Modification to trailing sand boxes
27/11/48 Fitting independent steam brake valves
Withdrawn w/e 11/4/64

47478 Repairs	
3/4/30-24/4/30LS	59,663
6/4/31-9/5/31HG	19,973
26/7/32-12/8/32LS	30,985
21/3/34-17/4/34HS	41,903
6/1/36-30/1/36HG	45,516
28/5/37-26/7/37HS	47,790
7/5/39-29/5/39HG	53,767
11/3/42-28/3/42HS	74,332
29/4/44-11/5/44HG	49,181
22/6/46-25/7/46LS	46,118
25/9/48-22/10/48HG	38,242 Derby
24/12/51-5/2/52HG	57,604 Derby
6/8/54-19/8/54HI	42,921 Derby
3/4/57-3/5/57HG	44,428 Derby

47478 Sheds	
Warrington	14/1/28
Devons Road	28/1/28
Swansea	21/4/34
Upper Bank	5/5/34
Swansea East Dock	5/9/59
Wolverton Wks	10/10/59
Birkenhead	24/2/62
Wolverton Wks	17/3/62
Nuneaton	7/7/62
Stafford	6/4/63
Nuneaton	25/5/63
Stored serviceable 11/11/62-31/3/63	

47478 Boilers	
No.6812	29/5/39
No.7858	11/5/44
No.10234	22/10/48
No.6831	5/2/52
No.14312	3/5/57

47479

Built as 16562 at The Vulcan Foundry Ltd 12th January 1928
Works No.4181
Renumbered 7479 14/9/34; 47479 w/e 15/1/49
21/4/34 Vacuum control gear
6/3/36 Fitting cast iron piston rod packing [experiment]
6/3/36 Fitting cup leather type of piston packing
11/6/38 Bell communication
11/6/38 Manually operated blow down valves
25/12/43 Regulator handle extension
25/12/43 Fitting steel in lieu of copper boiler tubes
10/8/57 Modified pistons for continuous blow down valves
Withdrawn w/e 4/8/62

47479 Repairs	
7/10/29-25/10/29LS	48,644
10/9/30-24/9/30LS	31,248
5/6/31-11/7/31HG	19,639
13/3/33-23/3/33LS	42,300
28/8/34-14/9/34HS	34,239
17/2/36-6/3/36HG	38,710
29/3/38-6/6/38HS	66,683
27/7/40-10/8/40HG	63,245
17/10/42-4/11/42HS	47,586
24/11/43-24/12/43HS	30,097
5/3/46-21/3/46HG	45,519
8/12/48-11/1/49HI	57,429 Derby
7/12/50-26/1/51HG	34,986 Derby
23/7/54-11/8/54HI	58,812 Derby
8/7/57-9/8/57HG	35,916 Derby

47479 Sheds	
Warrington	14/1/28
Devons Road	28/1/28
Swansea	14/4/34
Upper Bank	5/5/34
Crewe South	25/12/48
Upper Bank	1/1/49
Swansea East Dock	5/9/59
Wolverton Wks	10/10/59
Crewe South	24/2/62
Wolverton Wks	17/3/62
Nuneaton	7/7/62

47479 Boilers	
No.7489	10/8/40
No.7850	24/12/43
No.7524	21/3/46
No.10581	26/1/51
No.10232	9/8/57

47480

Built as 16563 at The Vulcan Foundry Ltd. 12th January 1928
Works No.4182
Renumbered 7480 23/4/34; 47480 w/e 24/12/49
3/11/34 Vacuum control gear
29/10/38 Manually operated blowdown valves
29/10/38 Bell communication
24/1/42 Regulator handle extension
24/1/42 Fitting steel in lieu of copper boiler tubes
Withdrawn w/e 2/10/65

47480 Repairs	
27/11/29-19/12/29LI	42,637
7/3/31-31/3/31LO	26,836
26/7/31-15/8/31HG	8,063
27/9/32-11/10/32LS	30,517
12/11/34-10/12/34HG	51,398
14/1/37-25/1/37LS	65,684
31/8/38-10/10/38HG	53,789
21/9/40-5/10/40HS	55,972
1/12/41-3/1/42HS	33,948
6/12/43-18/12/43LS	49,894
24/11/45-8/12/45HG	49,931
10/2/48-8/3/48LS	49,669 Derby
25/11/49-21/12/49HG	39,683 Derby
11/9/52-13/10/52HI	50,403 Derby
28/3/55-25/4/55HG	45,141 Derby
31/7/61-18/9/61HG	87,879 Derby

47480 Sheds	
Warrington	21/1/28
Devons Road	28/1/28
Swansea	21/4/34
Upper Bank	5/5/34
Walton	30/3/57
Bank Hall	4/10/58
Aintree	10/3/62
Newton Heath	21/3/64
Stored serviceable 9/6/58-29/9/58 13/11/63-16/3/64	

47480 Boilers	
No.7550	10/10/38
No.11138	3/1/42
No.6775	8/12/45
No.8029	21/12/49
No.13625	25/4/55
No.13300	18/9/61

Life and Times of 47479 2. Still as 16562, at Crewe after some form of repair but prior to repainting, clearly. The occasion will be the fitting of the vacuum control gear in April 1934. Rail Archive Stephenson.

Life and Times of 47479 3. As one of the Swansea motor engines, at Swansea Paxton Street shed on 22 July 1956. Vacuum controlled regulator gear was fitted to 16560-16564 (7477-7481) in 1934 for motor trains; the engines were stationed at Upper Bank and worked out of Swansea St Thomas and Victoria stations. 'The external manifestation of the push/pull gear was a cylinder and rodding on the left-hand side of the smokebox, with vacuum created by the existing ejectors' as noted in Part One. The engines carried the 87K plate of Swansea Paxton Street, Upper Bank (their 'proper' home) being an uncoded sub-shed. K.C.H. Fairey, ColourRail

Life and Times of 47479 4. Fallen from grace on the Swansea locals, 47479 found itself one of the Wolverton works shunters before a final brief posting to Nuneaton. It seems to have done some work there; witness it standing inside the shed on 5 September, withdrawn a few days before but still bearing a local target. Since its days at Swansea it has lost the old LTS destination board brackets above the front buffer beam. Peter Groom.

Motor fitted (for South Wales) 47480 at Derby MPD after attending the works for a Heavy General, on 24 April 1955. 87K Swansea Paxton Street plate. Destination board brackets from the old days in East London retained. So these particular 0-6-0T 'shunters' managed passenger trains in different areas widely separated in time and in this they were unique. R.J. Buckley, Initial Photographics.

On tour. 47480 at Gwaun-Cae-Gurwen on 2 July 1955. It was hauling the two coach SLS Swansea District rail tour that day. Courtesy the amazing website *Six Bells Junction, The Railtour Files* we know that the tour involved another Jinty, 47477 and an 0-6-2T 5657, and ran from Swansea St Thomas to Port Talbot General by the sort of diverse ways then possible in South Wales. Every detail is available on *The Railtour Files*.

47481

Built as 16564 at The Vulcan Foundry Ltd. 12th January 1928
Renumbered 7481 2/8/35; 47481 w/e 14/10/50
26/3/34 Vacuum control gear
28/10/37 Bell communication
28/10/37 Manually operated blowdown valves
4/9/43 Fitting steel in lieu of copper boiler tubes
Withdrawn w/e 30/3/63

47481 Repairs		
12/11/29-4/12/29LS	44,917	
19/1/31-5/2/31LO	66,917	
17/4/31-6/5/31LS	71,792	
2/2/32-20/2/32HG	88,940	
10/4/33-24/4/33LS	30,212	
6/3/34-26/3/34HS	54,515	
6/7/35-3/8/35HG	34,030	
14/10/37-28/10/37LS	67,809	
13/2/39-16/3/39HG	103,782	
14/5/41-28/5/41HS	63,002	
12/8/43-24/8/43HG	56,743	
11/1/46-23/1/46LS	49,981	
10/3/48-8/4/48HS	42,404	Derby
11/9/50-9/10/50LI	42,779	Derby
3/5/54-31/5/54HG	58,769	Derby
24/1/57-18/2/57LI	44,855	Derby
2/4/60-9/6/60HG	44,349	Derby

47481 Sheds	
Warrington	21/1/28
Devons Road	28/1/28
Swansea	31/3/34
Upper Bank	18/5/34
Lancaster	28/3/59
Kingmoor	2/2/63

47481 Boilers	
No.7838	16/3/39
No.6790	28/5/41
No.7854	24/8/43
No.7852	8/4/48
No.13649	31/5/54
No.14121	9/6/60

47482

Built as 16565 at The Vulcan Foundry Ltd. 12th January 1928
Works No.4184
Renumbered 7482 12/3/35; 47482 w/e 12/11/49
28/9/37 Fitting light shield to sliding fire doors
28/9/37 Manually operated blowdown valves
3/12/49 Fitting Wakefield patent fountain type lubricator
Withdrawn w/e 22/10/66

47842 Repairs		
28/2/30-21/3/30LS	44,827	
18/3/31-11/4/31LO	21,745	
26/10/31-18/11/31HG	79,193	
27/6/32-1/7/32LO	14,360	
23/8/33-5/9/33LS	27,013	
2/8/34-21/8/34LO	23,926	
7/2/35-12/3/35HS	10,646	
13/2/36-18/2/36LO	26,360	
23/6/36-3/7/36LS	11,096	
2/9/37-28/9/37HG	30,127	
5/10/38-17/10/38LO	24,587	
29/12/38-11/1/39HS	3,816	
14/10/39-27/10/39LO	17,736	
22/2/40-10/4/40LO	6,769	
28/11/40-21/12/40LO	11,460	
6/10/41-15/10/41LO	13,903	
3/6/42-25/7/42HS	13,445	
5/7/43-13/7/43LO	17,336	
10/7/44-29/7/44LS	17,055	
20/8/45-30/8/45LO	15,967	
21/6/46-9/7/46LO	13,856	
21/1/47-8/3/47HG	10,705	Derby
9/2/48-18/2/48LO	16,312	Shed
13/1/49-24/1/49LC	14,623	Shed
22/10/49-11/11/49LI	12,900	Bow
27/6/51-27/7/51HG	24,321	Bow
26/9/54-8/10/54LC	45,467	Shed
7/3/55-7/4/55HG	6,804	Bow
17/11/59-11/1/60HG	65,651	Derby
14/1/64-14/4/64HI	-	Darlington

47482 Sheds	
Warrington	21/1/28
Devons Road	4/2/28
Barrow	23/1/57
Willesden	14/12/57
Crewe South	29/10/60

47482 Boilers	
No.7904	16/9/37
No.7861	25/7/42
No.5491	8/3/47
No.13641	27/7/51
No.13325	7/4/55
No.14389	11/1/60

47481 in active mood at its home shed Lancaster Green Ayre, on 2 September 1962. The motor gear would have become inoperable by now. 47469 next to it had only ever been at Lancaster. K.C.H. Fairey, ColourRail

47481 in company with 47281 at Kingmoor MPD in the early 1960s. Both were withdrawn in March 1963 and 47481 had only just got to Carlisle a few weeks before – it may be that it did little, or no work. Rail Archive Stephenson.

7482 before the War, on GN commuter work. This is probably the High Barnet terminus itself (note the headboard) with the engine ready to return to town. Rail Archive Stephenson.

47482 in its final Willesden days on 5 June 1960, with the destination boards we have just seen in use when the engine was a regular sight for GN commuters. Interesting to reflect that the Jinties' eventual successors on such work were Brush Type 2s! 47482 appears to have charge of the depot stores van. Peter Groom.

Renumbered Darlington-style, 47482 working as one of the pilots at Crewe in the summer of 1964. Beyond, framed by two ancient smokeboxes, stands an electric locomotive. RailOnline

47482 amid the shadows at Crewe station. ColourRail

Out in the light now at Crewe station, in the summer of 1964. Darlington's insistence on placing the large (10 inch) number centrally on the tanks meant shifting the emblem up somewhat. The engine carried the North London destination board brackets from back in the mists of time to the end. RailOnline

47483

Built as 16566 at The Vulcan Foundry Ltd. 12th January 1928
Works No.4185
Renumbered 7483 1/4/36; 47483 w/e 12/8/50
18/5/40 Fitting Wakefield patent fountain type lubricator
27/12/41 Manually operated blowdown valves
Withdrawn w/e 3/3/62

47483 Repairs	
17/10/29-14/11/29LI	43,847
28/11/30-12/12/30LO	23,200
21/5/31-11/6/31LS	12,001
27/6/32-16/7/32HG	26,977
2/8/33-22/8/33LS	31,404
12/2/35-28/2/35HS	41,769
25/8/35-4/9/35LO	12,487
21/2/36-1/4/36HG	12,331
16/6/37-5/7/37LS	29,066
25/2/38-4/3/38LO	16,164
15/12/38-6/1/39LS	17,732
24/6/39-15/7/39HS	10,390
11/1/40-20/1/40LO	11,491
3/5/40-18/5/40HS	4,163
9/12/40-24/12/40LO	7,058
21/11/41-26/12/41HG	22,255
26/10/42-6/11/42LO	14,715
22/10/43-7/11/43LS	15,507
8/11/44-17/11/44LO	17,745
19/6/45-28/7/45HS	8,328
3/5/47-17/6/47HS	28,736 Bow
22/7/48-31/7/48LO	20,242 Shed
11/4/49-22/4/49LC	10,636 Bow
3/7/50-11/8/50HG	17,926 Bow
10/9/51-21/9/51LC	17,841 Bow
22/1/53-16/2/53LC	21,627 Shed
6/1/55-4/2/55HG	23,657 Bow
13/7/59-24/9/59LI	65,349 Bow

47483 Sheds	
Warrington	21/1/28
Devons Road	4/2/28
Willesden	8/3/58
Lancaster	5/11/60

47483 Boilers	
No.6866	26/12/41
No.6786	28/7/45
No.8089	11/8/50
No.14105	4/2/55

47484

Built as 16567 at The Vulcan Foundry Ltd. 12th January 1928
Works No.4186
Renumbered 7484 22/1/35; 47484 w/e 12/3/49
14/8/35 Fitting improved seal and axlebox lubrication pipes [experiment]
24/2/40 Fitting Wakefield patent fountain type lubricator
24/2/40 Manually operated blowdown valves
Withdrawn w/e 18/2/61

47484 Repairs	
27/3/30-10/4/30LS	59,042
23/2/31-13/3/31LS	25,184
19/11/31-5/12/31HO	15,553
4/5/32-1/6/32LS	8,943
23/6/33-5/7/33LS	28,275
26/11/34-22/1/35HG	32,623
23/7/35-14/8/35LO	13,890
28/2/36-4/3/36LO	27,409
4/6/36-18/6/36LS	4,948
11/3/37-19/3/37LO	17,611
5/5/37-19/3/37LO	49,968
10/11/37-24/11/37LS	14,313
26/12/38-4/1/39LO	25,940
5/1/40-2/2/40HG	22,962
14/4/41-28/4/41LO	16,026
2/5/42-13/5/42LO	20,441
18/6/42-4/7/42HS	1,835
22/5/43-1/6/43LO	21,032
12/5/44-9/6/44HS	20,508
10/11/45-19/11/45LO	23,066
17/2/47-19/3/47HS	24,176 Bow
15/3/48-27/3/48LO	25,201 Shed
7/3/49-22/3/49LC	17,353 Shed
22/9/49-24/10/49HG	9,769 Derby
8/11/49-9/11/49NC	869 Bow
16/11/50-27/11/50LC	22,167 Shed
22/1/51-15/2/51NC	3,556 Bow
9/11/51-23/11/51LC	- Bow
3/8/52-12/9/52HI	26,164 Bow
28/12/52-21/1/53NC	- Bow
25/9/53-15/10/53LC	20,077 Shed
23/7/54-16/8/54LC	15,720 Shed
11/3/55-25/3/55LC	12,154 Shed
5/11/55-13/1/56HG	5,701 Bow
1/12/58-19/12/58LC	59,627 Shed
6/1/59-23/1/59LC	- Shed

47484 Sheds	
Warrington	21/1/28
Devons Road	11/2/28
Plaistow	28/5/38
Devons Road	22/1/44
Plaistow	23/3/46
Tilbury	31/10/59

47484 Boilers	
No.6857	2/2/40
No.11674	9/6/44
No.13316	24/10/49
No.10580	13/1/56

7484 (47484) in its time on the LTS; location is probably Plaistow MPD. Cab awaits the lower rain strip. Rail Archive Stephenson.

47485

Built as 16568 at The Vulcan Foundry Ltd. 12th January 1928
Works No.4187
Renumbered 7485 14/4/36; 47485 w/e 30/4/49
10/5/32 clips for coal slacking pipes
Withdrawn w/e 9/1/65

47485 Repairs	
20/3/30-4/4/30LS	43,997
2/6/31-16/6/31LS	27,284
19/4/32-10/5/32HG	18,846
22/6/33-3/7/33LS	31,757
27/9/34-15/10/34HS	32,748
16/8/35-23/8/35LO	25,714
16/1/36-14/4/36HG	37,263
8/7/37-23/7/37LS	29,516
25/1/38-18/2/38LO	12,667
8/2/39-18/2/39LO	22,467
12/6/39-23/6/39LS	7,858
8/2/40-15/2/40LO	14,032
18/3/41-10/5/41HG	18,364
19/3/42-28/3/42LO	15.872
25/3/43-1/4/43LO	18,853
26/8/43-4/9/43LS	7,712
23/8/44-6/9/44LO	18,141
1/5/46-24/5/46HS	29,638
29/3/49-25/4/49HI	76,403 Derby
2/1/50-24/1/50LC	19,340 Derby
15/10/51-21/11/51HG	47,011 Derby
31/1/55-17/2/55LI	80,248 Derby
17/12/57-9/1/58HG	70,163 Derby

47485 Sheds	
Warrington	28/1/28
Devons Road	11/2/28
Nottingham	16/6/45
Burton	15/3/52
Leicester Mid	6/2/60
Kentish Town	4/3/61
Bedford	17/3/62
Wellingborough	3/8/63
Edge Hill	9/11/63
Stored serviceable 29/7/63-28/10/63	

47485 Boilers	
No.7886	10/5/41
No.7823	24/5/46
No.13978	21/11/51
No.10581	9/1/58

47486

Built as 16569 at the Vulcan Foundry Ltd. 12th January 1928
Renumbered 7486 24/1/36; 47486 w/e 1/5/48
29/1/36 Trial of C I piston rod packing [experiment]
29/1/36 Fitting light shields for sliding fire doors
15/6/40 Fitting Wakefield patent fountain type lubricator
22/2/41 Manually operated blowdown valves
Withdrawn w/e 12/3/60

47486 Repairs	
1/2/30-22/2/30LS	39,872
27/5/31-18/6/31HG	29,819
12/12/32-23/12/32LS	38,395
31/10/33-14/11/33LO	19,960
2/8/34-21/8/34LO	15,653
20/11/34-5/12/34LS	6,158
11/10/35-24/10/35LO	23,524
31/12/35-29/1/36HG	4,660
31/12/36-11/1/37LO	23,645
21/4/37-5/5/37LS	7,157
22/4/38-3/5/38LO	22,472
28/9/38-13/10/38LS	9,535
1/5/39-8/5/39LO	13,105
29/5/40-7/6/40LS	22,879
11/1/41-6/2/41HO	7,906
17/11/41-25/11/41LO	17,019
7/8/42-29/8/42LS	12,216
16/8/43-23/8/43LO	16,538
6/6/44-20/6/44HS	14,445
16/7/45-25/7/45LO	18,649
25/6/46-10/8/46HG	12,639
3/11/47-12/11/47LO	21,475 Shed
8/4/48-26/4/48NC	7,276 Bow
31/12/48-14/1/49LC	11,999 Shed
12/5/49-10/6/49HI	5,104 Bow
25/9/51-23/10/51HG	36,942 Derby
5/11/51-6/11/51NC	642 Bow
28/7/55-9/9/55HG	55,645 Bow

47486 Sheds	
Warrington	28/1/28
Devons Road	18/2/28
Wellingborough	7/10/39
Devons Road	9/12/39
Barrow	23/11/57
Willesden	14/12/57
Stored unserviceable 24/10/59-12/3/60	

47486 Boilers	
No.7487	10/8/46
No.13965	23/10/51
No.14108	9/9/55

47485 at Bedford, 20 March 1963; the difference in appearance imparted by the bottom rain strip (see previous picture) is quite marked. RailOnline

47486 at Willesden MPD. The year would be 1960 when the engine was withdrawn – note absence of shed plate and generally knocked-about condition and its abandonment on an out of the way siding. Its final Heavy General was in 1955, which meant it retained the first emblem to the end. Twenty or more Jinties had gone the previous year (1959) and thereafter attrition would proceed at the rate of about one a week. At one time they were being *delivered* at a faster rate than that. Rail Archive Stephenson.

47487

Built as 16570 at the Vulcan Foundry Ltd. 12th January 1928
Works No.4189
Renumbered 7487 18/12/35; 47487 w/e 12/3/49
14/1/36 Trial of CI piston rod packing [experiment]
14/1/36 Fitting fountain type lubricators
Withdrawn w/e 21/8/65

47487 Repairs	
10/4/30-2/5/30LS	47,512
24/11/31-11/12/31HG	37,331
13/7/32-19/7/32LO	15,407
14/8/33-26/8/33LS	27,865
9/7/34-30/7/34LO	23,134
18/12/34-11/1/35LS	11,264
17/12/35-14/1/36HG	24,526
3/11/36-18/11/36LO	31,266
10/5/37-10/6/37LO	13,129
26/5/38-13/6/38HS	23,682
21/6/39-28/6/39LO	23,373
8/4/40-4/5/40HG	17,168
23/5/41-5/6/41LO	17,135
5/5/42-14/5/42LO	32,631
26/8/42-8/9/42LS	5,461
26/5/43-3/6/43LO	11,874
18/5/44-21/8/44HS	17,939
5/10/45-13/10/45LO	17,560
21/1/46-2/3/46HS	4,271
7/2/47-22/2/47LO	16,574 Shed
7/11/47-17/11/47LO	12,506 Shed
28/1/48-21/2/48NC	3,562 Bow
6/9/48-23/9/48LO	8,445 Shed
7/2/49-7/3/49HI	- Bow
27/12/50-5/1/51LC	30,963 Bow
7/3/53-10/4/53HG	51,807Derby
12/1/57-30/1/57LI	99,848 Derby
11/4/60-10/6/60HG	78,902 Derby

47487 Sheds	
Devons Road	no date
Edge Hill	6/1/51

47487 Boilers	
No.6555	4/5/40
No.6562	2/3/46
No.14043	10/4/53
No.12688	10/6/60

47488

Built as 16571 at the |Vulcan Foundry Ltd. 12th January 1928
Works No.4190
Renumbered 7488 31/3/36; 47488 w/e 18/2/50
24/1/42 Manually operated blowdown valves
25/3/50 Fitting Wakefield patent fountain type lubricator
Withdrawn w/e 1/12/62

47488 Repairs	
22/4/30-9/5/30LS	53,223
1/6/31-25/6/31HG	23,048
5/9/32-15/9/32LS	32,733
10/9/34-25/9/34LS	47,040
10/10/34-16/10/34LO	316
1/8/35-9/8/35LO	18,364
2/1/36-31/3/36HG	8,562
23/2/37-4/3/37LO	22,391
5/7/37-22/7/37LS	8,594
4/3/38-12/3/38LO	15,167
14/12/38-6/1/39LS	17,123
28/12/39-11/1/40LO	20,991
29/1/40-2/3/40HS	868
Damaged-Enemy Action Devons Rd 10/10/40	
2/4/41-18/4/41LO	17,779
26/12/41-19/1/42HG	12,087
13/10/42-24/10/42LO	13,871
23/10/43-1/11/43LO	18,231
29/1/44-15/2/44LS	3,952
6/3/45-21/3/45LO	18,115
4/6/46-16/6/46LO	18,614
11/1/47-19/2/47HS	9,575 Derby
13/3/48-23/3/48LO	19,822 Shed
9/2/49-17/3/49LC	16,951 Bow
23/1/50-14/2/50HI	15,886 Bow
12/12/52-30/1/53HG	49,773 Bow
27/1/56-2/3/56HG	42,586 Bow
5/5/58-22/5/58HG	36,404 Derby

47488 Sheds	
Warrington	28/1/28
Devons Road	11/2/28
Edge Hill	19/10/57

47488 Boilers	
No.11092	19/1/42
No.5949	19/2/47
No.6749	30/1/53
No.7534	2/3/56
No.13637	22/5/58

Edge Hill's 47487 in the depths of Liverpool dockland, 13 June 1964. 1T90 denotes a rail tour, confirmed by the Swinging Sixties Undergraduate figure fixing the LUPTS board on the buffer beam – Liverpool University Public Transport Society. ColourRail

A Jinty on the North London line. Devons Road's 47488 comes through Caledonian Road & Barnsbury station, 17 August 1957. RailOnline

47489

Built as 16572 at the Vulcan Foundry Ltd. 12th January1928
Works No.4191
Renumbered 7489 8/1/36; 47489 w/e 15/1/49
13/1/36 Trial of C I* piston rod packing [experiment]
13/1/36 Fitting light shields for sliding fire doors
13/1/36 Fitting fountain type lubricators
15/6/40 Manually operated blowdown valves
25/11/44 Fitting steel in lieu of copper boiler tubes
*cast iron
Withdrawn w/e 19/12/59

47489 Repairs	
16/10/29-4/11/29LS	43,904
6/1/31-20/1/31LS	31,849
26/10/31-20/11/31HG	19,412
6/2/33-17/2/33LS	33,473
3/4/34-18/4/34HS	28,762
2/7/34-23/7/34LO	5,178
11/6/35-18/6/35LO	23,184
16/12/35-13/1/36HG	13,857
1/1/37-19/1/37LO	33,958
25/5/37-11/6/37LS	7,628
30/3/38-12/4/38LO	20,239
18/11/38-1/12/38LS	13,283
27/11/39-7/12/39LO	22,974
18/5/40-2/6/40HS	9,248
27/6/41-8/7/41LO	17,792
18/6/42-8/7/42LO	18,153
31/10/42-13/11/42HS	6,556
30/8/43-6/9/43LO	14,882
14/8/44-17/11/44HG	17,448
11/1/46-18/1/46LO	18,773
29/5/47-31/7/47LO	shed
24/3/48-5/4/48LO	12,381 Shed
10/11/48-13/1/49HG	- Bow
21/1/50-10/2/50LC	18,329 Shed
11/12/50-23/12/50LC	32,387 Shed
11/12/52-30/12/52LI	83.823 Derby
25/5/55-7/7/55HG	66,695 Derby

47489 Sheds	
Warrington	28/1/28
Devons Road	18/2/28
Edge Hill	6/1/51
Stored unserviceable 18/10/58-19/12/59	

47489 Boilers	
No.7610	2/6/40
No.7515	17/11/44
No.7809	13/1/49
No.11556	7/7/55

47490

Built as 16573 at the Vulcan Foundry Ltd. 1st February 1928
Works No.4192
Renumbered 7490 4/7/34; 47490 w/e 28/1/50
20/1/36 Fitting fountain type lubricators
25/2/38 Manually operated blowdown valves
Withdrawn w/e 13/7/63

47490 Repairs	
1/5/30-16/5/30LS	50,011
6/2/31-19/2/31LO	19,559
12/10/31-3/11/31HG	16,080
27/6/32-1/7/32LO	18,727
17/2/33-3/3/33LS	18,789
13/6/34-11/7/34HS	34,565
8/8/35-21/8/35LO	32,037
1/9/35-20/9/35LS	1,097
11/8/36-27/8/36LO	23,681
7/1/37-21/1/37LS	11,731
15/11/37-22/11/37LO	20,304
5/2/38-25/2/38HG	5,598
26/8/38-23/9/38LO	14,467
18/2/39-2/3/39LO	11,001
2/5/39-9/5/39HS	4,130
25/3/40-3/4/40LO	20,896
24/12/40-10/1/41HS	12,621
1/12/41-12/12/41LO	15,318
17/9/42-23/9/42LO	15,545
27/2/43-24/3/43HG	8,615
6/3/44-14/3/44LO	17,646
18/12/44-17/1/45LS	12,182
25/11/46-16/12/46LO	28,529 Shed
4/8/47-11/9/47HS	9,376 Bow
24/7/48-6/8/48LO	15,033 Shed
17/3/49-25/3/49LC	25,374 Bow
13/12/49-27/1/50HG	12,993 Derby
30/11/50-8/12/50LC	13,772 Bow
19/2/53-16/3/53HI	50,037 Bow
8/6/56-5/7/56HG	56,496 Derby
29/2/60-29/3/60HI	62,487 Derby

47490 Sheds	
Warrington	11/2/28
Devons Road	18/2/28
Speke Jct	3/10/53
Widnes	6/10/56
Sutton Oak	23/9/61

47490 Boilers	
No.7544	15/2/38
No.7167	24/3/43
No.7560	27/1/50
No.11674	5/7/56

Edge Hill's 47489, not long arrived from Devons Road and yet to acquire a cast front number plate (the East London works, as mentioned, curiously lacking the ability to make them) at work as Liverpool Lime Street pilot in 1951. Rail Archive Stephenson.

47490, still with first emblem, in the yard at its home shed Sutton Oak in 1963, the year of its withdrawal. RailOnline

47491

Built as 16574 at the Vulcan Foundry Ltd. 1st February 1928
Works No.4193
Renumbered 7491 14/1/35; 47491 w/e 12/1/52
Withdrawn w/e 15/12/62
24/3/32 Clips for coal slacking pipes
3/11/35 Fitting Wakefield fountain type lubricators for axleboxes
11/11/37 Manually operated blowdown valves

47491 Repairs	
16/2/30-14/3/30LS	47,878
23/2/31-17/3/31LO	22,160
8/3/32-24/3/32HG	23,098
20/7/32-26/7/32LO	8,318
9/1/34-23/1/34LS	39,298
9/11/34-15/1/35HG	21,926
27/1/36-3/2/36LO	23,342
30/12/36-15/1/37LS	24,994
20/10/37-11/11/37HS	19,219
24/11/38-2/12/38LO	26,750
24/4/39-8/5/39HS	10,830
4/6/40-18/6/40HS	24,816
10/7/41-23/7/41LO	17,824
20/6/42-30/6/42LO	15,672
29/10/42-11/11/42LS	7,215
15/11/43-22/11/43LO	20,506
7/11/44-30/12/44HG	16,375
6/3/46-16/3/46LO	19,726
22/4/47-14/5/47LO	19,008 Shed
11/2/48-18/3/48HS	14,566 Bow
28/2/49-11/3/49LC	19,014 Bow
8/4/49-10/5/49NC	1,401 Bow
3/12/51-10/1/52HG	47,863 Derby
10/8/55-13/9/55LI	66,972 Bow
3/5/58-28/5/58HG	29,800 Derby

47491 Sheds	
Warrington	11/2/28
Devons Road	18/2/28
Willesden	17/12/49
Uttoxeter	14/4/56
Nuneaton	3/11/56
Wrexham Rhosddu	10/11/56
Patricroft	8/11/58

47491 Boilers	
No.7813	2/11/37
No.6562	18/6/40
No.7873	30/12/44
No.10586	10/1/52
No.13639	28/5/58

47492

Built as 16575 at the Vulcan Foundry Ltd. 2nd February 1928
Works No.4194
Renumbered 7492 31/10/35; 47492 w/e 25/2/50
30/12/32 Fitting clips for coal slacking pipes
1/11/35 Fitting light shields for sliding fire doors
22/2/36 Fitting fountain type lubricators
21/12/36 Strengthening driving axleboxes by means of welded strips [experiment]
9/10/37 Fitting independent steam brake valves
9/10/37 Manually operated blowdown valves
Withdrawn w/e 25/7/64

47492 Repairs	
27/1/30-14/2/30LS	40,149
9/2/31-5/3/31HS	23,455
20/1/32-11/2/32LS	25,194
11/12/32-30/12/32HO	17,814
30/1/34-12/2/34LS	24,241
11/2/35-28/2/35LO	17,814
7/9/35-1/11/35HG	30,010
2/9/36-9/9/36LO	12,452
8/12/36-21/12/36LS	7,424
20/9/37-9/10/37HO	17,340
10/2/38-24/2/38LS	8,922
11/10/38-20/10/38LO	16,289
28/8/39-8/9/39LS	21,064
27/7/40-5/8/40LO	19,511
7/8/41-30/8/41HG	14,434
3/8/42-13/8/42LO	17,777
20/9/43-30/9/43LO	20,493
15/7/44-30/9/44HS	20,304
12/9/45-24/9/45LO	14,809
13/8/46-5/9/46LO	14,134
20/2/47-8/4/47HS	7,531 Bow
22/4/48-30/4/48LO	21,641 Shed
4/4/49-11/4/49LC	15,598 Bow
28/1/50-21/2/50HI	13,327 Bow
12/7/50NC	6,790 Bow
25/5/52-17/7/52HG	31,503 Bow
16/11/55-12/12/55HI	49,884 Derby
12/7/57-24/7/57LC	22,352 Shed
13/6/59-9/7/59HG	51,278 Derby

47492 Sheds	
Warrington	11/2/28
Devons Road	18/2/28
Cricklewood	11/10/47
Devons Road	20/12/47
Willesden	2/5/53
Kingmoor	15/3/58

47492 Boilers	
No.7860	11/10/35
No.7686	4/10/37
No.6673	30/8/41
No.11087	8/4/47
No.13987	17/7/52
No.6843	9/7/59

7491 heads north on the GN having just cleared Finsbury Park. As touched upon in Part One, it was never intended that the new tanks should be restricted to shunting, far from it and from the first they were seen as useful replacements for the old North London 4-4-0Ts, for instance: *Lest the 3F tanks be remembered only as 'shunters' it can be noted that plenty of passenger work came their way at first. Easily the most remarkable was their employment from 1927 on North London workings out of Broad Street over the LNER branches to Edgware, Alexandra Palace and High Barnet and the main line to Potter's Bar and Hatfield in place of North London 4-4-0Ts. Sadly a photograph of a Jinty racing a Gresley Pacific has yet to surface.* The lines to the right lead off to High Barnet and Alexandra Palace. Rail Archive Stephenson.

Without any indication as to where 47491 might be, it would take a true genius to identify this particular precise location. Yet all is not lost. The 84K shed plate narrows down the period, having been invented for the old GC Wrexham Rhosddu shed in February 1958. 47491 took its leave for Patricroft at the end of that year so there we have the year, while it's reasonable to state that this scene is 'the Wrexham area'...

Almost toy-like with its ancient bird cage stock, 16575 (7492, 47592) powers north through Greenwood, heading north about 1930. Rail Archive Stephenson.

47492 at Kingmoor MPD in the early 1960s; it is almost certainly the 'coal stage pilot' and will shortly be dealing with that run of coal wagons. Beyond is the steam breakdown crane shed. RailOnline

47493 has found itself at Warrington Dallam MPD on 1 May 1965, its home shed plate, 8F Springs Branch, hanging by a single bolt – an interrupted theft maybe!? To the north is the Folly Lane bridge (the shed entrance was a ramp down there, out of sight on the left) with the gas works beyond. RailOnline

47493

Built as 16576 at the Vulcan Foundry Ltd. 3rd February 1928
Works No.4195
Renumbered 7493 17/6/35; 47493 w/e 6/11/48
12/7/38 Manually operated blow down valves
12/7/38 Fitting Wakefield patent fountain type lubricator
Withdrawn w/e 31/12/66
Engine preserved

47493 Repairs	
15/5/30-30/5/30LS	43,927
11/5/31-5/6/31HG	25,813
29/8/32-9/9/32LS	36,804
1/2/34-13/2/34LS	34,828
11/9/34-26/9/34LO	17,158
22/5/35-20/6/35HG	15,879
30/4/36-6/5/36LO	25,614
8/1/37-22/1/37LS	17,620
15/12/37-28/12/37LO	22,872
15/6/38-12/7/38HS	10,075
4/8/39-14/8/39LO	25,978
29/11/39-8/12/39LS	6,147
12/8/40-21/8/40LO	15,058
22/8/41-9/9/41LO	14,005
29/10/41-11/11/41LS	2,498
13/8/42-22/8/42LO	13,911
12/9/43-13/10/43HG	14,987
12/10/44-20/10/44LO	19,259
22/9/45-13/10/45LS	15,003
15/11/46-4/12/46LO	19,998 Shed
27/1/48-14/2/48LO	18,214 Bow
29/9/48-5/11/48HS	11,509 Derby
9/7/51-24/7/51LC	45,974 Shed
6/12/51-29/12/51HI	- Bow
25/1/52-13/2/52NC	34,465 Bow
1/3/54-8/4/54HG	30,966 Bow
22/9/58-9/10/58HI	67,893 Derby
10/4/61-29/5/61HG	39,115 Derby

47493 Sheds	
Warrington	11/2/28
Devons Road	18/2/28
Speke Jct	6/11/54
Newton Heath	13/12/58
Speke Jct	14/3/59
Springs Branch	21/7/62
Edge Hill	4/9/65

47493 Boilers	
No.7473	4/7/38
No.7565	13/10/43
No.11667	5/11/48
No.6848	8/4/54
No.13973	29/5/61

47494

Built as 16577 at the Vulcan Foundry Ltd. 3rd February 1928
Works No.4196
Renumbered 7494 18/4/35; 47494 w/e 4/9/48
25/4/35 Fitting light shields for sliding fire doors
21/5/39 Fitting Wakefield patent fountain type lubricator
21/5/39 Manually operated blowdown valves
Withdrawn w/e 22/10/66

47494 Repairs	
2/12/29-21/12/29LS	45,754
29/12/30-13/1/31LS	21,675
2/9/31-23/9/31HG	17,284
16/6/32-22/6/32LO	20,123
10/11/32-25/11/32LS	29,820
19/10/33-6/11/33HS	22,748
18/9/34-3/10/34LO	22,345
13/3/35-25/4/35HG	11,311
14/3/36-23/3/36LO	26,857
10/8/36-25/8/36LS	10,617
20/7/37-5/8/37LO	21,899
19/10/37-4/11/37HS	5,129
30/7/38-9/8/38LO	16,361
21/4/39-10/5/39HG	16,633
24/4/40-2/5/40LO	20,940
26/12/40-8/1/41LS	11,857
26/4/41-25/5/41LO	5,258
20/4/42-27/4/42LO	16,726
7/5/43-17/5/43LS	18,878
13/5/44-19/5/44LO	19,039
6/2/45-10/3/45HG	8,727
16/2/46-8/3/46LO	13,673
1/4/47-19/4/47LO	19,709 Shed
11/8/47-19/9/47LO	5,785 Bow
10/6/48-31/8/48HS	13,771 Bow
18/7/51-31/8/51HI	49,851 Bow
27/8/53-1/10/53LC	31,640 Shed
5/6/54-9/7/54HG	11,705 Bow
14/7/58-15/8/58LI	62,335 Derby
12/7/61-22/9/61HG	48,847 Derby

47494 Sheds	
Warrington	11/2/28
Devons Road	18/2/28
Barrow	20/7/57
Monument Lane	19/10/57
Crewe South	8/12/62
Crewe Works	17/8/63
Crewe South	14/12/63

47494 Boilers	
No.7566	10/5/39
No.8058	10/3/45
No.6884	31/8/48
No.13306	9/7/54
No.14050	22/9/61

The familiar early combination of 6 inch letters and 8 inch numbers, with the space reserved for the emblem-to-come. The engine is at Derby MPD and the occasion would be its Heavy Service overhaul at the end of 1948. Rail Archive Stephenson.

47495 below the unmistakable hanging lights of Willesden MPD. It is ready for washing out, possibly, the plug covers being off, but is in a very tired state. It had a Heavy General in 1958, which would have seen the first emblem replaced; this is probably that very year, when the engine was based a little way up the line at Camden. J. Sutton, ColourRail

47495

Built as 16578 at the Vulcan Foundry Ltd. 7th February 1928
Works No.4197
Renumbered 7495 14/11/35; 47495 w/e 4/12/48
15/6/40 Manually operated blowdown valves
14/7/45 Fitting Wakefield patent fountain type lubricator
Withdrawn w/e 25/9/65

47495 Repairs	
11/12/29-10/1/30LS	47,482
16/1/31-20/1/31LS	24,607
20/10/31-31/10/31LO	18,466
23/2/32-12/3/32HG	7,496
28/7/32-12/8/32LO	10,753
8/6/33-21/6/33LS	22,749
11/6/34-28/6/34HS	27,000
24/4/35-13/5/35LO	19,008
29/10/35-16/11/35HG	14,802
8/9/36-17/9/36LO	23,330
22/1/37-3/2/37LS	8,417
25/10/37-29/11/37LO	16,241
26/7/38-18/8/38HS	14,675
14/8/39-2/8/39LO	24,296
30/4/40-20/5/40HS	13,343
26/6/41-5/7/41LO	16,862
15/6/42-24/6/42LO	16,907
27/8/42-9/9/42LS	4,545
28/6/43-5/7/43LO	14,254
25/8/44-4/9/44LO	21,603
8/6/45-30/6/45HG	16,010
12/12/46-31/12/46LO	24,144 shed
18/8/47-23/9/47HS	10,931 Derby
6/11/48-3/12/48NC	18,983 Bow
14/12/48-4/1/49LC	702 Shed
13/1/50-28/2/50HG	16,270 Derby
15/3/50-16/3/50NC	969 Bow
27/2/53-2/4/53HG	47,546 Bow
15/8/55-16/9/55LI	33,185 Bow
14/3/58-14/5/58HG	36,338 Bow

47495 Sheds	
Warrington	11/2/28
Devons Road	25/2/28
Camden	12/4/58
Bidston	9/1/60
Birkenhead	9/2/62

47495 Boilers	
No.5816	20/5/40
No.6445	30/6/45
No.7527	28/2/50
No.13955	2/4/53
No.14380	14/5/58

47496

Built as 16579 at the Vulcan Foundry Ltd. 7th February 1928
Works No.4198
Renumbered 7496 2/8/34; 47496 w/e 6/9/52
2/3/37 Fitting continuous blowdown apparatus
2/3/37 Fitting bonded asbestos fibre for packing gauge frames [experiment]
14/7/45 Fitting Wakefield patent fountain type lubricator
Withdrawn w/e 30/11/63

47496 Repairs	
13/3/30-28/3/30LS	44,930
15/5/31-29/5/31LO	28,621
4/8/31-29/8/31LS	4,926
15/2/32-24/2/32LO	12,702
16/9/32-18/10/32HS	11,082
6/7/34-1/8/34HS	41,881
30/9/35-14/10/35LO	33,005
17/10/35-7/11/35HS	33,005
5/8/36-19/8/36LO	23,073
23/1/37-2/3/37HG	13,683
22/3/38-31/3/38LO	30,434
19/7/38-29/7/38LS	7,502
18/7/39-27/7/39LO	24,100
20/6/40-8/7/40HS	20,523
22/6/43-10/7/43LS	43,314
9/1/45-18/1/45LO	29,512
15/6/45-7/7/45HG	7,440
31/8/48-3/9/48LO	51,709 Shed
20/5/49-22/6/49LI	12,293 Bristol
23/7/52-27/8/52HG	38,571 Derby
6/11/56-22/11/56HG	60,289 Derby

47496 Sheds	
Warrington	11/2/28
Devons Road	25/2/28
Cricklewood	26/4/41
Devons Road	18/12/43
Bath Green Park	30/6/45

47496 Boilers	
No.7504	8/7/40
No.6787	7/7/45
No.7887	27/8/52
No.14293	22/11/56

Bath's 47496 provides a marked contrast to 47495, working near Derby station on 1 December 1956 after a Heavy General overhaul at the works nearby. Note bracket on bunker for the Whitaker tablet exchanger in use on the S&D. The original blue S&D 'Bagnalls' (see 22 and 23 for instance in Part One, page 5) had these brackets on the tank side, ahead of the doorway. It is December, but that tarpaulin will not be flapping about on the long journey home to Bath – it will stay here in Derby. R.J. Buckley, Initial Photographics.

Back home. 47496 at Radstock MPD in the early 1960s. It was on the S&D without further works attention for six more years until withdrawal. Down here in the sticks, shunting and banking, its daily mileages would not have been inordinately high. The metal hook hanging off the smokebox door was used by the guard leaning out from the brake van of a goods train to uncouple from the engine at the top of the bank. Rail Archive Stephenson.

47497

Built as 16580 at the Vulcan Foundry Ltd. 3rd April 1928
Works No.4199
Renumbered 7497 31/10/35; 47497 w/e 5/2/49
20/4/40 Fitting Wakefield patent fountain type lubricator
20/4/40 Manually operated blowdown valves
16/6/46 fitting steel in lieu of copper boiler tubes
10/8/57 Modified pistons for continuous blowdown valves
Withdrawn w/e 22/9/62

47497 Repairs	
18/1/30-7/2/30LS	44,680
8/12/30-23/12/30LS	19,681
16/4/31-9/5/31HG	7,514
2/6/32-15/6/32LS	29,364
28/3/34-17/4/34HS	44,158
14/3/35-8/4/35LO	22,412
14/10/35-1/11/35HG	12,870
15/9/36-24/9/36LO	25,976
12/1/37-26/1/37LS	8,450
17/1/38-26/1/38LO	24,353
24/8/39-2/9/39LO	24,575
10/2/40-6/4/40HG	9,620
15/5/41-29/5/41LO	19,970
28/1/42-12/2/42LS	11,886
7/12/42-18/12/42LO	15,187
31/12/43-26/1/44HS	19,882
16/5/45-31/5/45LO	20,251
20/4/46-18/5/46HG	14,673
2/2/48-21/2/48NC	30,782 Bow
11/7/48-24/7/48LO	6,388 Shed
5/1/49-31/1/49HI	37,509 Bow
10/2/50-25/2/50LC	17,821 Shed
15/9/51-22/10/51HG	39,520 Derby
6/11/51NC	882 Bow
6/4/55-29/4/55LI	50,560 Bow
14/6/57-19/7/57HG	28,456 Bow

47497 Sheds	
Warrington	7/4/28
Devons Road	21/4/28
Kingmoor	23/8/58
Birkenhead	23/11/58

47497 Boilers	
No.7862	6/4/40
No.6808	18/5/46
No.13968	22/10/51
No.14207	19/7/57

47498

Built as 16581 at the Vulcan Foundry Ltd. 3rd April 1928
Works No 4200
Renumbered 7498 28/5/36; 47498 w/e 9/4/49
7/4/32 Clips for coal slacking pipes
28/5/36 Fitting hasps for retaining cab windows in open position [experiment]
31/12/39 Fitting Wakefield patent fountain type lubricator
9/8/41 Manually operated blowdown valves
Withdrawn w/e 12/3/60

47498 Repairs	
8/5/30-23/5/30LS	47,472
17/6/31-10/7/31LS	28,185
16/3/32-7/4/32HG	18,462
22/8/32-25/8/32LO	11,768
11/5/33-23/5/33LS	19,758
21/11/34-6/12/34HS	37,667
22/8/35-29/8/35LO	16,121
21/4/36-28/5/36HG	16,267
11/5/37-3/6/37LS	26,775
13/6/38-23/6/38LS	26,155
23/5/39-2/6/39LO	22,468
12/12/39-21/12/39HS	11,381
15/6/40-24/6/40LO	10,968
1/7/41-23/7/41HG	27,535
8/6/42-6/7/42LO	14,985
14/7/43-21/7/43LO	17,093
22/4/44-6/5/44LS	13,871
4/9/45-18/9/45LO	23,184
2/7/46-5/8/46HS	12,472
27/10/47-7/11/47LO	20,603
6/11/48-27/11/48LO	11,102
14/3/49-7/4/49LI	- Bow
17/1/52-11/2/52HG	50,128 Derby
13/10/55-27/10/55LI	94,101 Derby

47498 Sheds	
Warrington	7/4/28
Devons Road	21/4/28
Edge Hill	6/1/51
Stored serviceable 16/7/38-26/7/38	
Stored unserviceable 21/2/59-12/3/60	

47498 Boilers	
No.7480	23/7/41
No.7514	5/8/46
No.10239	11/2/52

47496, at Masbury on the S&D in the 'Big Freeze' of 1963. It had long been a Bath District engine, probably sub-shedded at Radstock, since the end of the War. Keith Miles sets the scene: *From both Radstock in the north and Evercreech Junction in the south, the line rose steeply for some seven or eight miles in each direction with long stretches at 1 in 50 to meet at the 811ft above sea level summit on the Mendip Hills between Binegar and Masbury. The terrain was such that many freight trains required to be banked. Initially the bank engines stayed with the trains over the summit to be uncoupled at either Masbury or Binegar before returning whence they came. In later years, however, they were uncoupled by the guard short of the summit (The 3-link couplings of steam-braked engines were easier to lift off than heavier screw-couplings) but didn't stop and commence a return until the train's brake van had been seen to pass over the summit. They then ran 'wrong road' until the crossovers just short of Binegar and Masbury stations.* 47496, one of the Jinties normally used as a bank engine, is fitted with a snowplough and the 8F, Bath's 48660, was there presumably to give it an extra shove. www.transporttreasury*

47497 at its final home, Birkenhead, about 1960. This is the original LMS shed; the adjoining GW building is out of sight to the right. By this time the WR locomotives on the allocation had been eliminated. Rail Archive Stephenson.

47499

Built as 16582 at the Vulcan Foundry Ltd. 11th April 1928
Works No 4201
Renumbered 7499 14/7/36; 47499 w/e 6/8/49
11/11/37 Fitting light shield to sliding fire doors
11/11/37 Manually operated blowdown valves
25/1/41 Fitting Wakefield patent fountain type lubricator
25/1/41 Regulator extension handle
Withdrawn w/e 28/8/65

47499 Repairs	
6/1/30-23/1/30LS	42,682
4/12/30-31/12/30LS	19,210
5/1/32-25/1/32LO	26,910
8/6/32-24/6/32LS	7,793
20/2/33-24/3/33HG	14,525
1/5/34-16/5/34LS	26,772
7/5/35-18/5/35LO	23,501
4/7/35-14/8/35LS	3,614
12/5/36-25/5/36LO	20,071
26/6/36-14/7/36LS	1,963
28/5/37-8/6/37LO	21,021
14/10/37-11/11/37HG	8,796
5/12/38-12/12/38LO	31,795
10/3/39-27/3/39HS	5,715
15/12/39-23/12/39LO	17,382
8/10/40-28/10/40LO	15,058
13/1/41-25/1/41LS	2,380
22/10/41-1/11/41LO	12,346
12/6/42-30/7/42HS	10,944
22/7/43-28/7/43LO	18,111
5/5/44-12/5/44LO	13,946
28/8/44-16/9/44LS	4,597
22/10/45-6/11/45LO	16,633
11/10/46-28/11/46HG	15,540 Bow
28/8/48-13/9/48LO	31,364 Shed
27/6/49-3/8/49HI	12,071 Bow
28/12/49-30/1/50HC	6,327 Derby
24/9/51-24/10/51HG	34,095 Derby
5/9/55-4/10/55HG	56,463 Bow
23/1/62-9/2/62HG	- Derby

47499 Sheds	
Warrington	14/4/28
Devons Road	26/1/30
Cricklewood	11/10/47
Devons Road	20/12/47
Nuneaton	9/11/57
Northampton	4/1/58

47499 Boilers	
No.7521	29/10/37
No.7955	30/7/42
No.6747	28/11/46
No.13972	24/10/51
No.14112	4/10/55

47500

Built as 16583 at the Vulcan Foundry Ltd. 13th April 1928
Works No 4202
Renumbered 7500 10/1/36; 47500 w/e 11/9/48
24/2/40 Fitting Wakefield patent fountain type lubricator
21/3/42 Manually operated blowdown valves
Withdrawn w/e 26/6/65

47500 Repairs	
18/6/30-4/7/30LS	53,168
27/4/31-20/5/31HG	20,859
24/10/32-4/11/32LS	37,682
17/5/34-5/6/34LS	37,228
8/6/35-17/6/35LO	26,165
18/7/35-26/7/35LO	2,586
2/12/35-10/1/36HS	9,662
2/1/37-4/2/37HG	26,043
3/2/38-12/2/38LO	31,055
31/8/38-14/9/38LS	13,087
19/9/39-4/10/39LO	23,217
6/2/40-17/2/40HS	7,925
Damaged-enemy action	
Devons Road 10/10/40	
25/10/40-2/11/40LO	9,428
7/4/41-23/4/41LO	12,272
4/2/42-21/3/42HG	14,305
22/2/43-27/2/43LO	17,355
22/11/43-16/2/44HS	14,399
30/3/45-16/4/45LO	48,612 ??
13/5/46-27/5/46LO	16,911
2/4/47-13/5/47HS	15,461 Bow
7/6/48-14/6/48LO	20,242 Shed
27/8/48-10/9/48NC	3,466 Bow
25/4/49-29/4/49LC	34,276 Bow
31/8/49-27/10/49HG	4,688 Bow
19/7/51-1/8/51LC	29,860 Bow
23/2/53-17/4/53HG	25,658 Bow
5/10/56-26/10/56LI	73,409 Bow
18/4/60-17/6/60HG	79,292 Derby

47500 Sheds	
Warrington	14/4/28
Devons Road	13/7/30
Bletchley	20/3/54
Wolverton Wks	26/9/59
Bletchley	23/4/60

47500 Boilers	
No.6811	21/3/42
No.5818	13/5/47
No.6741	27/10/49
No.14040	17/4/53
No.13731	17/6/60

47498 in contemporary numbering/lettering, at Devons Road in 1949. At this period, of the Devons Road allocation of about fifty engines, over forty were Jinties. There were only two tender engines, both 0-6-0s; the remainder of the complement comprised half a dozen or so 'North London' 0-6-0Ts which were the 'real' shunters, the Jinties being essentially trip engines. RailOnline

Barry Taylor, long-time correspondent for these series, writes: '47499 is an old friend – it is 1963 and it has somehow found itself in the middle of a rake of permanent-way wagons at Northampton Bridge Street Junction, with the eponymous signal box located just off picture to the left. The double track of the Blisworth-Peterborough branch runs across the foreground, with the eastern curve of the triangle surrounding the engine shed, and leading up to Castle station, veering off behind the temporary speed restriction sign. Northampton Bridge Street station, and its infamous level crossing, are away to the right; the Jinty is shunting sidings which form an extension of Bridge Street general coal and goods yard, whereas the Engineer's sidings, from which the wagons have probably originated, are on the opposite side of the line altogether. The bulk of Northampton gasworks looms large on the horizon, with the more attractive outline of the celebrated Brown & Pank wines and spirits warehouse hiding behind a crane; the latter was in the way of a new Carlsberg brewery, and would disappear, in a fire, a few years later. 47499 was a familiar sight around Northampton from January 1958, and would stay to the end of steam in the area in September 1965, spending its last few months stored outside the shed with another of the breed.' RailOnline

47500, long familiar on station pilot duty at Bletchley, in charge of vans at the east side of the station. This is its second period at Bletchley, 1960-65. Rail Archive Stephenson.

47501 at Devons Road Bow in 1949/50. It was there for a long time and only departed when the diesels began to arrive in 1957. It's worth noting that the displaced Devons Road Jinties did not go for scrap but went on to work elsewhere, often for several years. Next to 47501 is one of the North London 0-6-0Ts, of which there were still seven or eight at the shed in 1950. Collection Michael Boakes.

47501

Built as 16584 at the Vulcan Foundry Ltd. 13th April 1928
Works No 4203
Renumbered 7501 27/6/35; 47501 w/e 18/6/49
27/1/40 Fitting Wakefield patent fountain type lubricator
27/1/40 Manually operated blowdown valves
Withdrawn w/e 26/9/64

47501 Repairs	
25/6/30-11/7/30LS	57,457
23/11/31-12/12/31HG	33,343
16/6/32-23/6/32LO	12,777
16/1/33-27/1/33LS	18,635
2/11/33-15/11/33LS	24,853
19/10/34-29/10/34LO	23,874
31/5/35-27/6/35HG	15,408
9/5/36-19/5/36LO	25,410
3/12/36-14/1/37LS	14,172
14/1/38-22/1/38LO	22,637
26/4/38-9/5/38HS	5,574
30/12/38-12/1/39LO	14,951
15/12/39-26/1/40HG	19,499
20/2/41-3/3/41LO	18,682
29/1/42-14/2/42LS	14,204
19/12/42-30/12/42LO	21,427
15/12/43-23/12/43LO	12,656
7/7/44-10/8/44HS	9,364
22/9/45-5/10/45LO	18,070
19/8/46-31/8/46LO	14,940
20/12/46-17/2/47HG	5,836 Derby
16/2/48-25/2/48LO	18,123 Shed
22/12/48-14/1/49NC	15,695 Bow
11/4/49-2/5/49LC	37,982 Shed
4/5/49-17/6/49HI	- Bow
9/2/51-23/2/51LC	26,337 Bow
15/10/51-31/10/51LC	9,721 Bow
7/11/52-31/12/52HG	15,692 Bow
5/12/55-6/1/56LI	44,045 Bow
4/6/58-6/8/58HG	31,890 Bow

47501 Sheds	
Warrington	14/4/28
Devons Road	5/4/28
Barrow	23/11/57
Willesden	14/12/57

47501 Boilers	
No.5847	26/1/40
No.7876	17/2/47
No.13321	31/12/52
No.13955	6/8/58

47502

Built as 16585 at the Vulcan Foundry Ltd. 17th April 1928
Renumbered 7502 12/6/36; 47502 w/e 6/1/51
12/6/36 Fitting light shields for sliding fire doors
21/5/39 Fitting Wakefield patent fountain type lubricator
15/6/40 Manually operated blowdown valves
Withdrawn w/e 10/8/63

47502 Repairs	
7/5/30-23/5/30LS	47,963
20/4/31-2/5/31LO	22,839
16/12/31-30/12/31LO	16,200
22/1/32-9/2/32LS	1,840
26/10/32-21/11/32HS	14,196
3/8/34-5/10/34LS	43,279
24/9/35-11/10/35LO	25,441
6/5/36-12/6/36HG	11,826
7/6/37-17/6/37LO	26,696
4/2/38-19/2/38LS	17,197
3/2/39-15/2/39LO	27,690
15/4/39-29/4/39HS	4,069
31/1/40-7/2/40LO	19,925
22/5/40-4/6/40HS	6,034
7/7/41-18/7/41LO	16,803
23/5/42-6/6/42LS	15,212
3/6/43-15/7/43LO	15,876
22/9/43-6/10/43LO	3,083
19/8/44-7/10/44HG	15,821
3/12/45-8/12/45LO	19,787
13/3/47-1/4/47LO	21,166 Shed
21/7/47-16/9/47HS	5,165 Bow
18/11/48-8/12/48LO	19,490 Shed
28/2/50-18/3/50LI	20,951 Leeds
11/12/50-2/1/51HI	17,052 Derby
10/4/52-1/5/52HG	29,192 Derby
29/7/54-20/8/54HG	48,134 Derby
25/5/56-12/6/56HG	33,022 Derby
9/4/59-21/5/59HG	55,275 Bow

47502 Sheds	
Warrington	21/4/28
Devons Road	15/6/30
Staveley	12/3/49
Bromsgrove	10/3/51
Burton	21/9/57
Leicester	6/2/60
Kentish Town	18/11/61
Gorton	21/7/62
Stored serviceable 26/8/57-16/9/57	

47502 Boilers	
No.6854	4/6/40
No.7554	7/10/44
No.7336	16/9/47
No.13990	1/5/52
No.7896	20/8/54
No.5482	12/6/56
No.11135	21/5/59

47501 at work in the sidings at Bletchley. It still carries the vacuum tank for the Hudd ATC gear.

47501 enjoyed a new seven-year lease of life not far away from Bow, at Willesden where it would in any case have been found many times over the years, on trips from East London. It stands 'by the canal' at Willesden MPD on 12 August 1963; the mystery feature is the circle of small holes distributed around the smokebox door. Peter Groom.

47502 at Bromsgrove on 2 October 1954; it worked on the Lickey from 1951 to 1957. A.G. Ellis, transporttreasury

A Kentish Town Jinty, 47502, at Clapham Junction on the Southern Region in June 1962. Mike King ponders: *Interesting, this one. The headcode is Cross-London Code No.3, which denoted Midland Lines and Clapham Junction or Victoria via Blackfriars Junction, so it has arrived via the spur from St.Pancras to the Metropolitan widened lines, Loughborough Junction and round through Battersea. As it is coupled to an LMS BGZ (six-wheeled passenger brake) I would think it has come round with either vans or milk tanks, but obviously cannot prove this. It is in the western end of platform 2 at Clapham Junction, so is perhaps about to return home, having delivered the tanks, etc. into the yard behind the brake. Maybe there was no return load. The shed plate has been removed and marked in chalk instead, presumably in view of its imminent departure to Gorton.* transporttreasury

47503

Built as 16586 at the Vulcan Foundry Ltd. 18th April 1928
Renumbered 7503 27/4/34; 47503 w/e 6/1/51
16/2/37 Independent steam brake valves
29/10/38 Manually operated blowdown valves
Withdrawn w/e 14/3/64

47503 Repairs	
19/11/29-10/12/29LS	54,014
7/4/31-4/5/31HG	36,022
11/3/33-23/3/33LS	43,698
27/3/34-27/4/34HS	27,759
8/12/36-16/2/37HG	71,345
18/5/39-24/6/39LS	57,555
17/9/41-1/10/41HG	61,746
30/11/43-16/12/43HS	55,412
29/3/47-30/4/47HG	65,003 Derby
9/12/50-1/1/51LI	54,890 Derby
31/12/52-4/2/53HG	29,171 Derby
20/1/58-7/2/58HG	58,682 Derby

47503 Sheds	
Warrington	21/4/28
Birkenhead Nth	5/5/28
Birkenhead	19/3/38
Carnforth	10/2/40
Oxenholme	15/11/41
Carnforth	6/9/47
Oxenholme	28/2/48
Barrow	12/4/58

47503 Boilers	
No.6864	16/2/37
No.9152	1/10/41
No.10535	30/4/47
No.7894	4/2/53
No.4036	7/2/58

47504

Built as 16587 at the Vulcan Foundry Ltd. 20th April 1928
Renumbered 7504 6/8/34; 47504 w/e 9/10/48
1/12/45 Fitting steel in lieu of copper boiler tubes
1/12/45 Modification to trailing sand boxes
26/3/55 Fitting independent steam brake valves
Withdrawn w/e 21/4/62

47504 Repairs	
15/10/29-15/11/29LS	52,157
15/5/31-29/5/31HG	42,511
18/3/33-3/4/33LS	44,614
16/7/34-6/8/34LS	29,350
18/1/36-29/1/36HG	35,498
19/4/38-23/5/38LS	59,366
1/6/40-24/6/40HG	44,124
23/6/43-3/7/43LS	70,545
17/1/45-10/2/45LO	43,690
29/10/45-13/11/45HG	17,186
8/9/48-6/10/48HS	74,62 Derby
18/12/51-10/1/52HI	85,893 Derby
3/3/55-24/3/55HG	80,253 Derby

47504 Sheds	
Warrington	21/4/28
Birkenhead Nth	5/5/28
Chester	9/5/42
Loaned to ROF Queensferry 25/12/43-28/12/43	
Holyhead	6/5/50
Chester	3/6/50

47504 Boilers	
No.7885	24/6/40
No.6868	13/11/45
No.6778	6/10/48
No.11880	24/3/55

Oxenhome's 7503, presumably on the daily pick-up, at Kendall on 3 August 1950. It was not renumbered until early 1951.
M.N. Bland, transporttreasury

47505

Built as 16588 at the Vulcan Foundry Ltd. 20th April 1928
Renumbered 7505 28/5/36; 47505 w/e 7/7/51
4/2/37 Fitting screw reversing gear
9/12/37 Manually operated blowdown valves
15/7/39 Fitting Wakefield patent fountain type lubricator
Withdrawn w/e 7/8/65

47505 Repairs	
2/10/29-14/10/29LS	50,178
11/11/31-23/11/31LS	58,392
23/1/33-6/2/33HG	31,422
16/4/35-30/4/35LO	44,995
23/7/35-28/8/35LS	10,157
14/5/36-28/5/36LO	16,701
23/1/37-4/2/37HS	15,901
3/11/37-9/12/37HG	16,776
29/12/38-8/1/39LO	26,600
4/7/39-15/7/39HS	13,352
27/6/40-5/7/40LO	28,410
17/12/40-11/1/41LS	6,706
5/1/42-15/1/42LO	17,702
5/6/42-6/7/42HO	6,631
1/12/42-24/12/42HG	6,182
3/12/43-8/12/43LO	18,936
13/12/44-11/1/45HS	15,178
3/1/46-19/1/46LO	13,340
11/9/46-29/9/46LO	10,347
30/8/47-20/9/47LO	14,185 Shed
20/1/48-2/3/48HS	5,545 Bow
14/3/49-23/3/49LC	19,658 Bow
7/6/51-6/7/51LI	58,502 Bow
9/12/54-31/12/54HG	62,427 Derby
28/2/60-1/4/60HG	73,225 Derby

47505 Sheds	
Warrington	21/4/28
Birkenhead	5/5/28
Devons Road	3/3/34
Willesden	17/12/49
Barrow	14/12/57
Crewe South	2/12/61
Crewe Works	6/7/63

47505 Boilers	
No.6792	26/1/33
No.6863	25/11/37
No.6870	24/12/42
No.7521	2/3/48
No.14102	31/12/54
No.13730	1/4/60

47506

Built as 16589 at the Vulcan Foundry Ltd. 24th April 1928
Renumbered 7506 25/1/36; 47506 w/e 8/5/48
20/1/36 Fitting fountain type lubricators
24/1/37 Fitting destination board brackets
14/6/41 Manually operated blowdown valves
Withdrawn w/e 12/3/66

47506 Repairs	
24/10/29-13/11/29LS	53,262
9/1/31-28/1/31LS	32,862
25/4/32-10/5/32HG	31,553
4/8/33-22/8/33HS	35,013
20/9/34-5/10/34LS	25,613
4/9/35-16/9/35LO	22,627
19/3/36-24/4/36HG	12,294
24/3/37-2/4/37LO	23,420
6/1/38-18/1/38LS	19,536
16/1/39-23/1/39LO	22,378
8/11/39-21/11/39LS	17,001
19/4/40-30/4/40LO	8,695
25/4/41-20/5/41HG	16,040
29/12/41-23/1/42LO	10,469
28/4/42-5/5/42LO	14,069
12/4/43-8/5/43HS	16,594
20/5/44-29/5/44LO	20,377
3/5/45-17/5/45LO	15,718
14/8/45-28/9/45HS	3,395
20/12/46-17/1/47LO	19,205 Shed
17/12/47-27/12/47LO	21,667 Shed
24/3/48-5/5/48LS	4,631 Bow
14/5/49-25/5/49LC	21,160 Shed
14/8/50-8/9/50HG	33,414 Derby
11/2/53-4/3/53HI	69,537 Derby
17/9/55-7/10/55HG	69,260 Derby
3/5/58-8/5/58LC	- Gloucester
17/5/59-8/6/59LI	- Derby
8/4/61-19/5/61HG	26,719 Derby

47506 Sheds	
Warrington	21/4/28
Birkenhead	5/5/28
Devons Road	3/3/34
Staveley	12/3/49
Gloucester	1/5/54
Bromsgrove	23/2/63
Bath Green Park	30/11/63

47506 Boilers	
No.8090	20/5/41
No.7518	28/9/45
No.13622	8/9/50
No.11553	7/10/55
No.14052	19/5/61

47506, after some brief service as a Lickey banker, at Bath Green Park MPD on 24 July 1965. At Boxing Day 1965 a visitor noted twenty engines at the shed, one or two under repair, others clearly abandoned or at least, unlikely to work again. *The Railway Observer* noted that 'The general condition of the engines externally left much to be desired' which was as true of the shed roof as 47506! ColourRail

At some point during its time at Bath 47506 found itself under repair at Bristol Barrow Road which was presumably the nearest depot with a wheel drop. The rear wheelset has been removed and the Jinty rests on a four wheel 'dolly'. With the Jinty in that proverbial state 'WM' (Waiting Material – it could be a long wait!) the picture is particularly interesting if for no other reason than the area at the back of the shed, formerly given over to repair work, is so far as I'm aware, never been photographed before. The wheel drop itself was a few yards away out of sight to the right. A wonderfully scruffy patch of the universal MPD environment. RailOnline

47507

Built as 16590 at the Vulcan Foundry Ltd. 25th April 1928
Renumbered 7507 11/6/36; 47507 w/e 2/9/50
11/6/36 Removal of injector overflow gear
11/6/36 Fitting of independent steam brake valve 0-6-0 standard tank
28/2/38 Manually operated blowdown valves
28/11/42 Fitting steel in lieu of copper boiler tubes
28/11/42 Regulator extension handle
2/11/57 Modified piston for continuous blowdown gear
Withdrawn w/e 20/8/66

47507 Repairs	
28/3/30-15/4/30LS	-
17/11/31-3/12/31LS	95,535
13/5/33-25/5/33HG	31,627
19/5/36-11/6/36HS	68,101
31/1/38-28/2/38HG	42,728
29/6/40-12/7/40LS	51,239
7/10/42-7/11/42HG	50,830
19/3/45-18/4/45HS	56,939
30/1/48-11/3/48HG	48,005 Derby
1/8/50-30/8/50LI	57,887 Derby
24/1/54-16/2/54HG	67,640 Derby
6/10/57-21/10/57LI	69,094 Derby
18/2/61-7/4/61HG	62,045 Derby

47507 Sheds	
Warrington	26/4/28
Birkenhead Nth	19/5/28
Crewe	12/8/31
Mold Jct	25/5/32
Birkenhead Nth	5/5/34
Crew CME o/l	12/3/38
Birkenhead	19/3/38
Rhyl	28/4/62
Llandudno Jct	9/2/63
Chester	16/7/66

47507 Boilers	
No.6793	22/2/38
No.6740	7/11/42
No.7484	11/3/48
No.13976	16/2/54
No.13312	7/4/61

47508

Built as 16591 at the Vulcan Foundry Ltd. 27th April 1928
Renumbered 7508 18/6/35; 47508 w/e 31/3/51
1/9/31 Clips for coal slacking pipe
16/11/36 Removal of injector overflow gear
23/1/43 Regulator handle extension
23/1/43 Fitting plate to bunker rail to prevent coal spillage
23/1/43 Fitting steel in lieu of copper boiler tubes
21/4/51 Fitting independent steam brake valves
Withdrawn w/e 30/9/61

47508 Repairs	
1/11/29-25/11/29LS	53,895
3/8/31-1/9/31HG	42,961
29/5/35-19/6/35LS	91,218
3/11/36-16/11/36HG	35,480
14/12/39-3/1/40HS	80,455
1/12/42-12/12/42HG	67,350
20/10/45-9/11/45HS	76,265
25/2/48-7/4/48HG	56,869 Derby
24/2/51-29/3/51LI	56,656 Derby
10/3/53-21/4/53HG	40,626 Derby
18/11/57-4/12/57HG	92,028 Derby

47508 Sheds	
Warrington	28/4/28
Birkenhead Nth	12/5/28
Crewe	16/4/30
Newton Heath	1/11/30
Sowerby Bridge	6/12/47

47508 Boilers	
No.6826	2/12/42
No.12687	7/4/48
No.10534	21/4/53
No.13968	4/12/57

47507 at Llandudno Junction MPD in the period when it was resident there, 1963-1966. Perhaps the winds off the Irish Sea were fiercer than most, for 47507 has, very naughtily, a knocked-up wood arrangement to secure that tarpaulin. P. Chancellor, ColourRail

47508 at Sowerby Bridge MPD during 1956, in company with L&Y 2-4-2T 50752. The Jinty came here at the end of 1947 and remained until withdrawal in 1961. Michael Boakes Collection.

47508 running light near its Sowerby Bridge home. The period is before 1956, when the old Lanky shed passed to the North Eastern Region. Rail Archive Stephenson.

47509

Built as 16592 at the Vulcan Foundry Ltd. 27th April 1928
Renumbered 7509 18/12/35; 47509 w/e 21/10/50
25/6/31 Clips for coal slacking pipe
20/12/35 Fitting light shields for sliding fire doors
8/9/45 Regulator handle extension
8/9/45 Fitting steel in lieu of copper boiler tubes
8/9/45 Modification to trailing sand boxes
4/11/50 Fitting independent steam brake valves
Withdrawn w/e 10/12/60

47509 Repairs	
3/10/29-18/10/29LS	45,765
2/6/31-25/6/31HG	43,963
1/8/33-18/8/33HS	53,474
2/12/35-20/12/35HS	58,434
17/3/38-2/4/38HS	58,407
27/11/40-14/12/40HG	57,228
18/9/43-12/10/43HS	72,589
2/8/45-14/8/45HG	49,724
21/6/48-9/7/48LS	70,309 Leeds
20/9/50-17/10/50HG	40,414 Derby
24/8/54-15/9/54LI	80,489 Derby
4/2/57-19/2/57HG	43,863 Derby
30/11/60	- Gorton

47509 Sheds	
Warrington	28/4/28
Birkenhead	19/5/28
Crewe	14/4/30
Newton Heath	1/11/30
Sowerby Bridge	6/12/47

47509 Boilers	
No.6868	14/12/40
No.10023	14/8/45
No.13629	17/10/50
No.7828	19/2/57

47510

Built as 16593 at the Vulcan Foundry Ltd 1st May 1928
Renumbered 7510 5/12/36; 47510 w/e 1/10/4
25/4/32 Fitting locomotive rail washer (de-sanding)
25/4/32 Fitting clips to coal slacking pipe
3/12/36 Removal of injector overflow gear
8/10/49 Fitting independent steam brake valves
Withdrawn w/e 12/11/60

47510 Repairs	
8/10/29-25/10/29LS	40,595
29/10/30-7/11/30LS	19,699
5/4/32-25/4/32LS	32,790
8/12/33-6/1/34HG	38,629
18/2/35-21/3/35LO	28,950
29/10/36-3/12/36LS	41,906
6/1/39-3/3/39HG	52,764
7/5/42-29/5/42HS	79,865
16/11/42-19/12/42LO	12,629
20/7/44-1/8/44HG	42,729
25/8/47-25/9/47LS	83,406 Derby
8/9/49-30/9/49HG	42,204 Derby
12/12/53-15/1/54HG	90,636 Derby
11/2/58-27/2/58LI	91,232 Derby

47510 Sheds	
Warrington	3/5/28
Birkenhead Nth	26/5/28
Barrow	25/10/29
Longsight	16/4/30
Newton Heath	1/11/30
Sowerby Bridge	6/12/47
Wakefield	21/8/48
Sowerby Bridge	10/9/60

47510 Boilers	
No.6633	3/3/39
No.6823	1/8/44
No.10524	30/9/49
No.11084	15/1/54

47509 at Derby shed, possibly in 1954 after the Light Intermediate that year – given that it hasn't been repainted and the emblem has obviously been there a while. T.G. Hepburn, Rail Archive Stephenson.

47511

Built as 16594 at the Vulcan Foundry Ltd 2nd May 1928
Renumbered 7511 8/10/35; 47511 w/e 1/4/50
8/10/35 Fitting light shield for sliding fire doors
20/1/36 Fitting fountain type lubricator
13/7/40 Manually operated blowdown valves
13/7/40 Cooling down adaptor
Withdrawn w/e 18/4/64

47511 Repairs	
6/3/30-27/3/30LS	40,320
1/7/31-17/7/31LS	31,272
2/12/31-8/1/32HO	10,049
14/3/33-24/3/33LS	26,618
12/4/34-4/5/34HS	26,868
1/3/35-11/3/35LO	23,024
7/8/35-8/10/35HG	11,717
21/8/36-28/8/36LO	23,742
14/1/37-27/1/37LS	12,463
3/11/37-13/11/37LO	18,708
14/5/38-30/5/38LS	12,206
15/5/39-22/5/39LO	21,712
1/11/39-2/12/39LO	10,459
31/5/40-28/6/40HS	110,212
10/6/41-21/6/41LO	14,423
15/4/42-9/5/42LS	16,274
16/4/43-24/4/43LO	17,406
15/3/44-25/3/44LO	16,155
21/7/44-15/9/44HG	5,340
4/10/46-14/11/46LO	32,483 Shed
10/9/47-3/10/47HS	12,375 Derby
24/1/49-2/2/49LC	22,762 Shed
3/3/50-28/3/50LI	20,032 Bow
8/11/51-22/11/51LC	26,035 Derby
15/9/53-16/10/53HG	53,898 Derby
31/1/57-20/3/57HG	47,478 Bow
6/9/57-13/9/57NC	6,684 Bow

47511 Sheds	
Warrington	3/5/28
Devons Road	19/5/28
Bangor	9/11/57
Stored serviceable 10/2/63-18/4/64	

47511 Boilers	
No.6787	28/6/40
No.7525	15/9/44
No.7875	3/10/47
No.11669	16/10/53
No.14306	20/3/57

47512

Built as 16595 at the Vulcan Foundry Ltd 3rd May 1928
Renumbered 7512 14/4/36; 47512 w/e 13/8/49
7/5/32 Clips for coal slacking pipe
4/10/41 Manually operated blow down valves
4/10/41 Regulator handle extension
13/8/49 Fitting Wakefield patent fountain type lubricator
Withdrawn w/e 8/5/65

47512 Repairs	
10/7/30-25/7/30LS	42,232
8/7/31-30/7/31LS	24,042
29/4/31-12/5/31LO	62,180
10/4/32-7/5/32HG	20,821
14/6/33-23/6/33LS	30,183
24/9/34-10/10/34HS	35,219
16/11/34-27/11/34LO	1,956
14/9/35-19/9/35LO	25,192
1/2/36-14/4/36HG	9,161
17/4/37-29/4/37LO	26,226
5/7/37-16/7/37LS	2,575
15/2/38-24/2/38LO	13,673
27/3/39-5/4/39LO	25,054
20/6/39-4/7/39LS	4,129
3/7/40-12/7/40LO	23,300
25/8/41-20/9/41HG	23,288
20/3/44-14/4/44HS	54,155
6/2/47-18/3/47HG	62,823 Derby
25/3/48-3/4/48LO	22,939 Shed
4/4/49-12/4/49LC	22,245 Bow
16/7/49-8/8/49LI	5,461 Bow
30/9/50-24/10/50LC	24,708 Bow
15/6/51-6/7/51LC	12,885 Bow
7/7/52-15/7/52LC	23,470 Bow
29/12/52-6/2/52HG	9,450 Bow
16/3/53-27/3/54LC	24,579 Shed
25/1/55-3/2/55LC	15,387 shed
23/11/55-16/12/55LI	11,504 Bow
30/12/55NC	- Bow
23/3/56NC	- Bow
4/4/57-17/4/57LC	15,099 Shed
29/7/57-9/8/57LC	4,321 Bow
7/3/58-2/5/58HG	9,833 Bow
10/3/59-1/4/59LC	16,533 Shed
22/1/60-17/2/60LC	25,637 Shed

47512 Sheds	
Warrington	5/5/28
Devons Road	19/5/28
Tilbury	9/4/38
Plaistow	15/4/39
Belle Vue	29/8/42
Plaistow	23/3/46
Tilbury	28/11/59
Lower Darwen	7/1/61
Aintree	6/5/61
Stored serviceable 13/11/63-12/2/64 28/9/64-25/1/65	

47512 Boilers	
No.5818	20/9/41
No.5847	18/3/47
No.7819	6/2/52
No.14355	2/5/58

47513

Built as 16596 at the Vulcan Foundry Ltd 4th May 1928
Renumbered 7513 2/12/36; 47513 w/e 19/6/48
10/8/40 Manually operated blow down valves
Withdrawn w/e 13/5/61

47513 Repairs	
26/2/30-14/3/30LS	42,268
15/12/30-7/1/31LS	20,595
9/7/31-30/7/31HG	12,924
8/12/32-22/12/32LS	35,245
26/1/34-10/2/34HS	27,774
3/12/34-12/12/34LO	23,903
21/9/35-21/11/35HG	20,231
20/11/36-28/11/36LO	22,178
7/4/37-13/5/37LS	6,559
13/4/38-22/4/38LO	20,917
24/9/38-8/10/38LS	9,826
27/6/39-4/4/39LO	10,560
20/1/40-30/1/40LO	17,893
12/7/40-2/8/40HS	11,271
26/7/41-7/8/41LO	14,572
2/6/43-29/6/43LS	37,991
29/10/45-21/11/45HG	60,084
6/5/48-16/6/48HS	67,485 Bow
3/7/50-8/8/50HG	54,602 Derby
12/10/53-2/11/53LI	80,168 Derby
23/4/56-9/5/56HG	61,748 Derby

47513 Sheds	
Warrington	5/5/28
Devons Road	19/5/28
Grimesthorpe	7/3/41

47513 Boilers	
No.5805	2/8/40
No.5816	21/11/45
No.12048	8/8/50
No.13633	9/5/56

One of Grimesthorpe's finest, 47513 on duty at Sheffield Midland. It's not easy to tell the period; its last Heavy General was 'on the cusp' of the new emblem's introduction and it would have missed it. It could well have kept the original emblem till withdrawal. RailOnline

47514

Built as 16597 at the Vulcan Foundry Ltd 4th May 1928
Renumbered 7514 28/11/36; 47514 w/e 15/1/49
30/1/36 Trial of CI piston rod packing
23/5/40 Fitting Wakefield patent fountain type lubricator
25/1/41 Manually operated blow down valves
25/1/41 Cooling down adaptor
30/11/57 Modified piston for continuous blowdown valves
Withdrawn w/e 19/5/62

47514 Repairs	
11/2/30-1/3/30LS	39,899
15/12/30-10/1/31LS	20,778
27/4/31-20/5/31HG	7,926
29/12/32-9/1/33LS	45,898
29/6/34-17/7/34HG	32,744
29/6/35-13/7/35LO	23,796
8/1/36-30/1/36HG	11,806
21/1/37-2/2/37LO	26,438
16/3/37-7/4/37HS	29,910
26/1/38-3/2/38LO	19,168
19/5/38-2/6/38LS	6,639
25/2/39-6/3/39LO	15,812
5/3/40-21/3/40LS	23,946
23/12/40-20/1/41HG	24,010
4/11/41-12/11/41LO	14,317
7/11/42-18/1/42LO	34,021
24/2/43-6/5/43LS	38,507
9/10/43-25/4/44LO	11,598
30/6/44-14/7/44LO	3,080
26/5/45-18/6/45LO	12,952
2/3/46-2/4/46HS	15,269
14/6/48-25/6/48LO	38,555 shed
23/12/48-14/1/49HI	9,771 Bow
22/2/50-10/3/50LC	18,779 Bow
11/12/51-18/1/52HG	47,825 Derby
5/2/52-8/2/52NC	933 Bow
8/6/55-8/7/55HI	51,154 Bow
8/10/57-15/11/57HG	36,170 Bow

47514 Sheds	
Warrington	6/5/28
Devons Road	19/5/28
Camden	14/6/58
Carnforth	5/11/60

47514 Boilers	
No.7514	20/1/41
No.6860	2/4/46
No.13983	18/1/52
No.14317	15/11/57

47515

Built as 16598 at the Vulcan Foundry Ltd 8th May 1928
Renumbered 7515 6/3/36; 47515 w/e 2/10/48
16/4/32 Clips for coal slacking pipe
23/3/40 Manually operated blow down valves
6/10/45 Fitting Wakefield patent fountain type lubricator
10/8/57 Modified pistons for continuous blow down valves
Withdrawn w/e 11/7/64

47515 Repairs	
3/7/30-18/7/30LS	41,670
18/5/31-5/6/31LO	21,581
29/3/32-16/4/32HG	20,658
31/8/32-3/9/32LO	12,119
16/7/34-2/8/34LS	51,185
6/11/34-14/11/34LO	6,848
14/9/35-25/9/35LO	19,489
9/1/36-6/3/36HG	13,373
3/2/37-12/2/37LO	22,392
17/6/37-6/7/37LS	9,458
3/6/38-11/6/38LO	24,212
19/11/38-3/12/38LS	10,461
14/11/39-25/11/39LO	24,265
16/1/40-27/2/40HS	11,011
23/4/41-4/5/41LO	17,530
9/4/42-21/4/42LO	15,940
23/9/42-6/10/42HS	8,707
9/4/43-16/4/43LO	9,921
16/12/43-25/5/44HO	14,067
7/2/45-16/2/45LO	11,540
14/7/45-18/8/45HG	6,534
4/12/46-27/12/46LO	21,815 shed
19/11/47-15/12/47LO	15,138 shed
13/8/48-2/10/48HS	12,176 Derby
18/10/48-19/10/48NC	920 Bow
15/11/51-14/12/51HG	49,612 Bow
18/4/55-6/5/55LI	52,331 Bow
2/7/57-1/8/57HG	33,114 Bow
2/62	- Derby

47515 Sheds	
Warrington	10/5/28
Devons Road	19/5/28
Loan to Melbourne Military Railway 9/3/40-26/3/40	
Kingmoor	23/8/58

Boilers	
No.6782	27/2/40
No.5952	18/8/45
No.6828	2/1048
No.13974	14/12/51
No.4209	1/8/57

47516

Built as 16599 at the Vulcan Foundry Ltd 8th May 1928
Renumbered 7516 3/12/34; 47516 w/e 26/6/48
2/10/37 Manually operated blowdown valves
20/5/50 Fitting Wakefield patent fountain type lubricator
Withdrawn w/e 10/2/62

47516 Repairs	
30/5/30-20/6/30LS	44,992
9/4/31-2/5/31HG	16,694
3/3/33-15/3/33LS	42,376
10/9/34-3/12/34HS	33,954
31/10/35-17/11/35LO	23,705
9/4/36-29/4/36HS	8,357
7/4/37-16/4/37LO	22,981
7/9/37-2/10/37HG	9,807
31/10/38-10/11/38LO	?
4/3/39-20/3/39LS	?
23/10/39-3/11/39LO	17,035
19/8/40-10/9/40LS	17,881
22/9/41-2/10/41LO	16,243
28/8/42-3/10/42HG	16,016
27/9/43-4/10/43LO	18,999
15/6/44-30/6/44LO	12,848
4/1/45-8/3/45HS	8,992
27/4/46-13/5/46LO	19,431
5/12/46-9/1/47LO	11,382 Bow
5/8/47-5/9/47HS	10,526 Derby
30/4/48-22/6/48NC	11,611 Bow
8/7/48-23/7/48LO	279 shed
23/3/50-25/4/50LI	41,356 Bow
16/12/52-19/1/53HG	43,983 Bow
15/10/56-2/11/56HG	71,491 Derby
2/7/60-26/8/60HI	89,596 Derby

47516 Sheds	
Warrington	10/5/28
Devons Road	19/5/28
Speke Jct	3/10/53
Crewe South	21/8/54

47516 Boilers	
No.7565	27/9/37
No.6884	3/10/42
No.7682	5/9/47
No.11137	19/1/53
No.13634	2/11/56

47515 at the north end of Carlisle station in 1960, dealing with vans on a parcels train. Almost hidden on the left is an EE Type 4, revealed only by its headcode box 1S53. ColourRail

A citadel pilot regular, 47515 carries on its familiar duties at the great station in the early 1960s. Court Square, part of the fine approach to the station, lies beyond. RailOnline

47516 spent its life in Lancashire or East London before landing up at Crewe South, in 1954. It stayed until withdrawn in 1962. Inevitable coal on roof. RailOnline

47517

Built as 16600 at W Beardmore Ltd 25th January 1928
Renumbered 7517 29/9/36; 47517 w/e 27/11/43
18/3/29 Fitting light shields for sliding firedoors
4/10/36 Fitting screw reversing gear
18/6/39 Fitting Wakefield patent fountain type lubricator
12/7/41 Manually operated blowdown valves
13/7/57 Modified piston for continuous blowdown valves
Withdrawn w/e 27/6/64

47517 Repairs	
5/5/31-2/6/31HG	60,930
15/2/34-27/2/34LS	58,613
22/1/35-14/2/35LO	20,846
20/8/35-4/9/35LS	12,479
36/6/36-9/7/36LO	19,079
4/11/36-11/12/36HG	6,342
18/12/37-5/1/38HS	30,460
21/1/39-28/1/39LO	29,312
17/5/39-26/5/39HS	6,629
29/5/40-4/6/40LO	25,097
25/1/41-24/6/41HG	9,534
19/1/42-29/1/42LO	11,061
28/11/42-5/12/42LO	26,604
4/10/43-23/10/43LS	15,280
29/9/44-11/10/44LO	15,962
19/4/45-2/5/45LO	7,785
18/2/46-26/3/46HS	11,936
12/7/47-22/7/47LO	20,263 shed
26/6/48-26/7/48LO	19,135 shed
28/10/48-27/11/48HS	6,170 Bow
6/2/50-2/3/50NC	20,547 Bow
13/4/51-15/6/51HG	17,571 Bow
30/4/53-22/5/53HC	28,757 Derby
10/6/53-11/6/53NC	nil Bow
9/10/54-2/11/54LI	49,165 Bow
22/2/56-5/3/56LC	18,492 shed
23/5/57-21/6/57HG	35,911 Derby

47517 Sheds	
Tebay	28/1/28
Crewe	6/2/29
Devons Road	20/3/29
Barrow	23/8/58
Newton Heath	13/12/58
Barrow	14/3/59
Springs Branch	25/11/61
Stored serviceable 28/4/63-22/6/64	

47517 Boilers	
No.7487	24/6/41
No.6867	26/3/46
No.13642	15/6/51
No.11666	22/5/53
No.11669	21/6/57

47518

Built as 16601 at W Beardmore Ltd 27th January 1928
Renumbered 7518 13/3/35; 47518 w/e 15/10/49
15/3/35 Trial of 'Eboline' heat resisting black enamel
4/10/36 Fitting screw reversing gear
8/4/38 Manually operated blowdown valves
8/4/38 Fitting Wakefield patent fountain type lubricator
1/12/57 Modified piston for continuous blowdown valves
Withdrawn w/e 26/10/63

47518 Repairs	
3/2/31-25/2/31LS	56,085
4/1/32-18/1/32LO	17,132
1/1/33-17/1/33HG	19,269
21/2/35-15/3/35HS	53,530
31/3/36-4/2/36LO	25,742
30/6/36-10/7/36LS	9,768
9/6/37-21/6/37LO	22,543
7/3/38-8/4/38HG	17,703
24/4/39-1/5/39LO	27,897
30/6/39-14/7/39LS	4,616
2/5/40-11/5/40LO	18,423
1/3/41-25/3/41LO	12,732
3/6/41-14/6/41HS	3,224
13/3/42-24/3/42LO	14,041
19/3/43-25/3/43LO	17,763
11/3/44-6/5/44HS	19,278
30/6/45-9/7/45LO	18,629
17/9/46-25/11/46HS	19,208 Bow
27/2/47-12/4/47HO	3,239 Bow
5/3/48-15/3/48LO	16,815 Shed
14/4/49-28/4/49LC	23,379 Shed
21/9/49-13/10/49LI	7,210 Bow
31/7/51-14/9/51HG	31,993 Bow
26/3/55-22/4/55LI	53,233 Bow
5/10/57-5/11/57HG	37,707 Bow

47518 Sheds	
Carlisle	28/1/28
Devons Road	21/3/31
Nottingham	19/2/49
Devons Road	26/2/49
Barrow	23/11/57
Stafford	25/11/61

47518 Boilers	
No.7525	24/3/38
No.8055	6/5/44
No.10235	12/4/47
No.13960	14/9/51
No.14319	5/11/57

47517 still with Hudd ATC, at Devons Road Bow about 1958.

16600 (7517, 47517) during its first years at Devons Road Bow. It was once an enormous place with two separate buildings which obviously provided more accommodation than was needed. When modernised with coaling plant and so on, one of the buildings was simply demolished, leaving only a water tank at the rear. You have to love the lamp sprouting from the dome.

A familiar picture to mark the completion of dieselisation at Devons Road Bow – 'BR's first all-diesel depot'. 47517 was the last steam engine to leave the shed at the end of August 1958. It was an unlikely development and trip work did not perhaps offer the greatest 'value added' given the enormous first cost of the diesels; diagrams, distance, manning and so could be radically altered to take advantage of the diesels' attributes but they were largely stuck with the existing steam diagrams. This was 1958 and everyone was feeling their way. The traffic anyway declined inexorably (the place closed in 1964) and two of the three locomotive types making up the new allocation proved disappointing and they too were done away with early. It signalled the course the Modernisation Plan would take: 41 steam locomotives were replaced by 31 diesels of three wholly different types, each from a different manufacturer and employing two different transmission types.

Alistair F. Nisbet, writing of his charming picture way back in *British Railways Illustrated*, November 2004: *Lime Street Longueur*. 'Back in July 1963 I had been sent with a colleague to our employer's Liverpool offices and, after finishing for the day, decided to have a closer look at Lime Street station. There was quite a contrast in what was on offer – two Jinties on pilot duties and two of the early AC electric locos, E3077 and E3012, waiting for further duties to the south. Of the two 3Fs 47412 was well up to the buffer stops with empty stock while 47519 was clearly waiting for something to happen. This, however, did not seem likely to occur very soon – the driver walked off to refill his tea can while the young fireman took a rest on the front running plate, pondering his non-steam future perhaps. Alistair F. Nisbet.

47519

Built as 16602 at W Beardmore Ltd 1st February 1928
Renumbered 7519 7/6/35; 47519 w/e 8/10/49
5/9/42 Regulator handle extension
5/9/42 Fitting steel in lieu of copper boiler tubes
2/12/51 Fitting independent steam brake valves
Withdrawn w/e 2/10/65

47519 Repairs	
10/4/31-28/4/31LS	62,870
11/4/32-6/5/32LO	18,399
26/9/32-12/10/32HS	8,620
24/5/35-7/6/35LS	60,136
10/2/37-16/3/37HG	40,263
18/3/39-28/3/39LO	47,660
23/1/40-7/2/40LS	19,061
7/7/42-11/8/42HG	59,346
16/1/45-8/2/45HS	63,183
5/3/45-21/3/45LO	212
30/7/47-29/8/47HG	49,995 Derby
15/9/49-7/10/49LI	46,637 Derby
1/5/53-29/5/53HG	82,811 Derby
12/5/56-30/5/56HI	79,417 Derby
7/3/60-8/4/60HG	98,232 Derby

47519 Sheds	
Carlisle	11/2/28
Devons Road	24/4/29
Willesden	9/12/31
Bescot	27/11/37
Edge Hill	18/11/50

47519 Boilers	
No.5673	11/3/37
No.7841	11/8/42
No.6811	29/8/47
No.14042	29/5/53
No.12051	8/4/60

47520

Built as 16602 at W Beardmore Ltd 3rd February 1928
Renumbered 7520 23/11/36; 47520 w/e 21/8/48
23/11/36 Removal of injector overflow gear
23/11/36 Fitting of independent steam brake valve
27/11/38 Manually operated blowdown valves
20/2/43 Regulator handle extension
20/2/43 Fitting steel in lieu of copper boiler tubes
20/2/43 Fitting plate to bunker rails to prevent coal spillage
Withdrawn w/e 27/11/65

47520 Repairs	
20/11/29-5/12/29LS	47,397
23/10/30-11/11/30LS	21,473
25/8/31-4/9/31HG	13,297
4/7/32-1/8/32LO	19,990
26/3/33-13/4/33LO	17,286
18/10/34-1/11/34LS	36,908
26/10/36-23/11/36HG	43,371
23/8/40-13/9/40LS	87,577
28/12/42-26/1/43HG	48,160
12/10/45-1/11/45HS	57,333
13/10/47-13/11/47LO	35,018 Shed
15/6/48-18/8/48HG	8,662 Derby
10/9/51-28/9/51LI	61,167 Bow
8/11/54-9/12/54HG	55,543 Derby
26/4/60-23/6/60HG	71,545 Derby
3/7/61-10/8/61LC	15,096 Horwich

47520 Sheds	
Carlisle	1/2/28
Birkenhead Nth	27/3/29
Camden	12/8/31
Willesden	31/3/34
Barrow	14/12/57
Springs Branch	21/1/61
Barrow	4/2/61
Carnforth	10/3/62
Carlisle Canal	8/9/62
Bolton	22/6/63
Newton Heath	6/11/65

47520 Boilers	
No.5825	26/1/43
No.6781	18/8/48
No.14123	9/12/54
No.11134	23/6/60

In a fascinating historical episode, Camden's 16604 (7521, 47521) is working as shed pilot during the reconstruction and modernisation of the grand old London depot. This was the 'flagship' of the vast MPD modernisations wrought on the LMS before the War but there is very little photographically to record any of it. To complete the scene, the engine in front (which the Jinty seems to have charge of) is 6100 ROYAL SCOT. Rail Archive Stephenson.

From shed pilot to station pilot. 47521 found itself at Crewe South for a few months in 1966 and on 29 May was serving as pilot at the station. C.P. Stacey, Initial Photographics.

47521

Built as 16604 at W Beardmore Ltd 7th February 1928
Renumbered 7521 5/3/36; 47521 w/e 14/8/48
21/4/29 Fitted with carriage warming gear
30/8/37 Manually operated blow down valves
30/8/37 Independent steam brake valves
30/8/37 Removal of injectors overflow gear
28/11/42 Fitting steel in lieu of copper boiler tubes
28/11/42 Regulator handle extension
Withdrawn w/e 8/10/66

47521 Repairs	
4/12/29-21/12/29LS	47,926
17/2/31-4/3/31LS	28,677
21/12/31-15/1/32LO	17,101
17/6/32-22/7/32LO	10,634
25/2/33-9/3/33HG	15,587
25/2/36-5/3/36LS	76,906
17/8/37-30/8/37HG	38,151
20/2/40-14/3/40LS	55,636
23/9/42-12/11/42HG	72,936
4/5/45-26/5/45HS	67,759
3/7/48-14/8/48HG	64,162 Derby
7/4/51-9/5/51LI	74,013 Bow
20/9/54-12/10/54HG	72,954 Derby
13/4/57-9/5/57LI	56,905 Bow
24/5/57-7/6/57LC	87 Bow
4/7/57-12/7/57NC	603 Bow
12/10/61-17/11/61HG	88,950 Derby

47521 Sheds	
Carlisle	18/2/28
Crewe	27/3/29
Birkenhead Nth	24/4/29
Camden	12/8/31
Bletchley	5/1/35
Nuneaton	13/9/47
Bletchley	25/10/47
Stoke	17/7/65
Crewe South	1/1/66
Stoke	13/8/66

47521 Boilers	
No.6761	2/3/33
No.6739	23/8/37
No.6803	12/11/42
No.11557	14/8/48
No.10310	12/10/54
No.13306	17/11/61

47522

Built as 16605 at W Beardmore Ltd 10th February 1928
Renumbered 7522 15/12/34; 47522 w/e 19/2/49
14/3/29 Fitted with carriage warming gear
28/12/37 Independent steam brake valves
1/12/45 Fitting steel in lieu of copper boiler tubes
1/12/45 Modification to trailing sand boxes
Withdrawn w/e 4/8/62

47522 Repairs	
22/10/29-7/11/29LS	44,335
10/6/31-29/6/31LS	35,564
14/6/32-5/7/32LO	25,381
20/10/32-1/11/32LS	8,861
28/11/34-15/12/34HG	50,394
6/8/36-11/9/36LO	44,783*
13/5/37-28/5/37HS	14,456
25/11/37-28/12/37LO	10,714
25/3/40-8/4/40HG	56,936
24/6/43-2/7/43LS	28,382
25/10/45-9/11/45HG	75,604
9/10/48-30/10/48LO	65,943 Shed
8/1/49-15/2/49LI	2,490 Bow
12/12/51-11/1/52HG	66,927 Derby
31/5/56-29/6/56HG	99,243 Derby
1/8/56-8/8/56NC	1,472 Bow
23/9/59-17/11/59LI	65,929 Derby
*'whole cost due to damage in collision'	

47522 Sheds	
Carlisle	18/2/28
Crewe	25/2/28
Birkenhead Nth	20/3/29
Warrington	18/5/30
Patricroft	27/8/30
Camden	15/4/31
Bletchley	5/1/35
Willesden	11/9/36
Camden	2/10/37
Carnforth	5/1/60
Workington	16/9/61

47522 Boilers	
No.5829	8/4/40
No.6749	9/11/45
No.7482	11/1/52
No.14298	29/6/56

47523

Built as 16606 at W Beardmore Ltd 15th February 1928
Renumbered 7523 31/1/36; 47523 w/e 17/6/50
7/3/29 Fitting carriage warming gear
3/11/37 Manually operated blowdown valves
3/11/37 Independent steam brake valves
30/10/43 Fitting steel in lieu of copper boiler tubes
Withdrawn w/e 12/11/60

47523 Repairs	
30/4/30-8/5/30LS	45,625
15/12/31-19/1/32LS	35,237
11/9/33-30/9/33HG	53,405
27/1/36-31/1/36LS	80,305
2/10/37-3/11/37HG	50,250
17/6/40-29/6/40HS	66,493
11/10/43-21/10/43HG	80,496
14/2/47-19/4/47HS	74,291 Derby
5/5/50-16/6/50LI	67,944 Bow
16/9/53-13/10/53HG	78,395 Derby
8/7/57-6/9/57HI	82,948 Bow

47523 Sheds	
Carlisle	18/2/28*
Crewe	18/2/28*
Mold Jct	31/10/28
Upper Bank	13/3/29
Willesden	31/12/30
Crewe South	17/2/32
*same date on history card	

47523 Boilers	
No.6761	28/10/37
No.8059	29/6/40
No.7508	21/10/43
No.6770	19/4/47
No.10241	13/10/53

47524

Built as 16607 at W Beardmore Ltd 16th February 1928
Renumbered 7524 22/1/36; 47524 w/e 1/4/50
13/3/29 Fitting carriage warming gear
15/2/37 Independent steam brake valve
29/10/38 Manually operated blowdown valves
22/3/42 Regulator handle extension
22/3/42 Fitting steel in lieu of copper boiler tubes
Withdrawn w/e 26/9/64

47524 Repairs	
28/5/30-4/6/30LS	47,857
29/8/32-12/9/32LS	51,343
4/9/33-26/9/33HG	33,679
13/1/36-22/1/36LS	77,565
25/1/37-15/2/37HG	33,391
27/11/39-4/1/40LS	76,971
14/2/42-3/3/42HG	52,441
24/7/44-4/8/44LS	61,646
3/5/47-2/6/47HG	58,818 Derby
4/3/50-27/3/50LI	69,390 Derby
1/5/53-29/5/53HG	71,448 Derby
29/4/57-14/5/57LI	87,664 Derby
15/4/60-10/6/60HG	69,503 Derby

47524 Sheds	
Crewe	25/2/28
Longsight	21/11/28
Upper Bank	13/3/29
Willesden	31/12/30
Crewe South	17/2/32

47524 Boilers	
No.5800	9/2/37
No.7851	3/3/42
No.7901	2/6/47
No.14065	29/5/53
No.13985	10/6/60

7524 in Crewe station; it spent over thirty years at Crewe South and its scruffy state and the spare coupling on the running plate could indicate it was a works shunter at the time. The period might well be the first part of 1947; a Heavy General later that year would have resulted in a much better appearance. Rail Archive Stephenson.

No doubt about the location. Pilots meet at Crewe in the late 1950s. In the early years of that decade 47524 was only one of nearly twenty Jinties at Crewe South. RailOnline

47525

Built as 16608 at W Beardmore Ltd 24th February 1928
Renumbered 7525 19/12/34; 47525 w/e 18/3/50
19/5/29 Fitting carriage warming gear
8/6/36 Fitting independent steam brake valve 0-6-0 std tank
30/3/38 Manually operated blowdown valves
30/10/43 Fitting steel in lieu of copper boiler tubes
Withdrawn w/e 19/3/60

47525 Repairs	
12/1/32-29/1/32LS	60,770
3/5/33-19/5/33LS	23,819
4/12/34-19/12/34HG	29,889
28/4/36-8/6/36LO	28,991
15/3/38-30/3/38LS	33,518
27/12/39-6/1/40HG	29,655
24/9/43-9/10/43HS	60,232
16/6/44-29/6/44LO	11,374
2/2/45-14/2/45HS	12,084
5/8/47-8/9/47HS	54,300 Derby
20/2/50-17/3/50HG	40,845 Derby
6/2/53-26/2/53LI	51,895 Derby
22/2/54-18/3/54LC	17,564 Derby
2/3/56-29/3/56HG	49,564 Derby

47525 Sheds	
Warrington	25/2/28
Lancaster	28/11/28
Carnforth	28/9/35
Barrow	18/12/37
Oxenholme	19/2/38
Carnforth	6/9/47
Moor Row	8/11/47
Workington	31/7/54
Stored unserviceable 6/6/59-19/3/60	

47525 Boilers	
No.7815	6/1/40
No.7897	14/2/45
No.5490	17/3/50
No.12056	29/3/56

16608 (7525, 47525) out on the road with an impressive train of empties; in the early 1930s it was a Lancaster engine and the architecture and stonework certainly match that area. Rail Archive Stephenson.

47525 at Derby MPD, following one of its overhauls there when it was a Moor Row engine, 1947-1954. Rail Archive Stephenson.

47526

Built as 16609 at W Beardmore Ltd 24th February 1928
Renumbered 7526 22/1/37; 47526 w/e 4/6/49
22/1/44 Fitting steel in lieu of boiler copper tubes
18/6/49 Fitting independent steam brake valves
18/6/49 Modification to trailing sand boxes
Withdrawn w/e 1/12/62

47526 Repairs	
15/6/32-5/7/32LS	68,446
16/1/34-26/1/34HG	35,631
24/12/36-22/1/37LS	73,297
22/10/38-29/12/38HG	42,107
30/4/41-10/5/41LS	63,379
24/12/43-12/1/44HG	55,716
17/9/46-28/9/46LS	60,748
6/5/49-1/6/49HG	57,358 Derby
21/1/53-18/2/53HI	90,822 Derby
26/11/55-22/12/55HG	59,354 Derby
28/2/59-25/3/59LI	80,132 Derby

47526 Sheds	
Warrington	25/2/28
Lancaster	27/11/28
Carnforth	28/9/35
Holyhead	8/2/36
Crewe	4/11/39
Alsager	1/3/41
Crewe South	22/1/44

47526 Boilers	
No.7890	29/12/38
No.11873	12/1/44
No.5486	1/6/49
No.14127	22/12/55

47527

Built as 16610 at W Beardmore Ltd 28th February 1928
Renumbered 7527 22/6/36; 47527 w/e 4/9/48
28/2/38 Manually operated blowdown valves
14/3/29 Fitting carriage warming gear
18/4/43 Fitting steel in lieu of copper boiler tubes
6/9/52 Fitting independent steam brake valves
Withdrawn w/e 19/3/60

47527 Repairs	
30/9/30-10/10/30LS	45,698
27/4/32-21/5/32LO	38,268
12/9/32-22/9/32LS	8,956
23/8/33-26/9/33HG	21,628
9/6/36-22/6/36LS	70,086
2/10/37-19/10/37LO	32,372
2/2/38-28/2/38HG	7,281
2/1/40-6/2/40LO	44,370
26/7/40-7/8/40HS	10,854
26/2/43-23/3/43HG	62,168
8/8/46-9/9/46HS	65,456
2/8/48-4/9/48HG	39,531 Derby
24/6/52-18/7/52LI	92,341 Bow

47527 Sheds	
Carlisle	3/3/28
Plodder Lane	20/3/29*
Camden	20/3/29*
Watford	7/12/46
Camden	1/3/47
Kingmoor	19/4/58
Stored unserviceable 7/3/59-19/3/60	
*Same dates on History Card	

47527 Boilers	
No.4963	21/2/38
No.6832	23/3/43
No.6804	4/9/48
No.13311	15/6/55

47527 at Kingmoor about 1958. It seems never to have had the second emblem.

47528

Built as 16611 at W Beardmore Ltd 2nd March 1928
Renumbered 7528 3/7/37; 47528 w/e 12/6/48
5/12/33 Fitting carriage warming apparatus
14/5/37 Manually operated blowdown valves
9/8/52 Fitting independent steam brake valves
2/11/57 Modified piston for continuous blow down gear
Withdrawn w/e 19/3/60

47528 Repairs	
19/8/30-10/9/30LS	44,217
20/11/31-18/12/31LO	28,312
21/3/32-16/4/32LO	6,267
10/8/32-20/8/32LS	7,861
16/11/33-5/12/33HG	28,670
27/9/35-18/10/35LO	47,013
1/1/37-20/1/37LO	31,162
22/5/37-30/6/37HS	7,516
19/1/38-15/2/38LO	11,977
20/7/38-29/8/38HG	9,207
17/12/40-3/1/41LS	41,113
30/12/42-28/1/43HS	49,765
27/6/45-17/7/45HG	56,109
22/5/48-9/6/48LS	59,607 Derby
23/12/49-27/1/50HG	39,834 Derby
3/7/52-7/8/52LI	62,112 Derby
5/2/55-24/2/55HG	61,248 Derby
1/10/57-22/10/57LI	67,080 Derby

47528 Sheds	
Carlisle	10/3/28
Camden	17/4/29
Stoke	23/10/37
Longsight	5/11/38
Stored unserviceable 5/8/58-19/3/60	

47528 Boilers	
No.10230	29/8/38
No.7880	17/7/45
No.11880	27/1/50
No.10584	24/2/55

47529

Built as 16612 at W Beardmore Ltd 6th March 1928
Renumbered 7529 1/7/36; 47529 w/e 28/8/48
21/4/29 Fitting carriage warming gear
20/4/33 Clips for coal slacking pipe
30/5/38 Manually operated blowdown valves
10/7/43 Fitting steel in lieu of copper boiler tubes
21/3/53 Fitting independent steam brake valves
Withdrawn w/e 21/10/61

47529 Repairs	
1/7/31-22/7/31LS	63,200
17/12/31-12/1/32LO	10,297
30/3/33-20/4/33HG	30,158
24/6/36-24/7/36HS	73,510
6/5/38-30/5/38HG	41,407
17/1/40-21/2/40LO	39,502
31/10/40-23/11/40HS	16,893
23/6/43-3/7/43HG	61,687
26/10/43-27/11/43LO	7,215
30/4/47-7/6/47LS	87,561 Bow
11/6/47-16/6/47LO	12 Bow
7/7/48-27/8/48HG	24,686 Derby
23/1/53-25/2/53HG	80,254 Bow
12/11/56-20/12/56HG	32,267 Bow
15/7/58-1/8/58LC	52,629 Bow

47529 Sheds	
Carlisle	17/3/28
Camden	17/4/29
Crewe South	5/11/60

47529 Boilers	
No.10234	30/5/38
No.7337	3/7/43
No.6772	27/8/48
No.7611	25/2/53
No.10582	20/12/56

An extremely shabby Camden Jinty, 47529, in the south yard at Camden MPD – not exactly a flag-bearer for pilot work at Euston. To the left is the coal pusher fitted BR1D tender of one of the Holyhead Britannias, to the right the famous Roundhouse. R.C. Riley, www.trasporttreasury

47530

Built as 16613 at W Beardmore Ltd 8th March 1928
Renumbered 7530 3/8/36; 47530 w/e 26/2/49
3/8/36 Fitting of independent steam brake valve
3/8/36 Removal of injector overflow gear
3/10/42 Regulator handle extension
3/10/42 Fitting steel in lieu of copper boiler tubes
Withdrawn w/e 8/10/66

47530 Repairs	
23/10/30-10/11/30LS	56,252
23/7/31-4/9/31LO	17,263
9/1/32-4/2/32LO	8,181
15/6/32-27/6/32LS	9,632
30/8/33-28/9/33HG	27,555
25/3/34-13/4/34LO	12,159
20/7/36-3/8/36HS	54,974
4/4/38-16/5/38HG	45,090
17/1/40-6/2/40LS	37,043
14/9/42-26/9/42HS	65,504
3/11/44-18/11/44LS	53,300
11/1/46-5/2/46HG	26,970
5/2/49-24/2/49HI	57,175 Derby
5/2/53-4/3/53HG	75,299 Derby
31/10/56-15/11/56LI	49,340 Derby
5/3/60-6/4/60HG	54,869 Derby

47530 Sheds	
Carlisle	24/3/28*
Patricroft	24/3/28*
Warrington	19/5/28
Camden	19/5/29
Birkenhead	11/8/34
Mold Jct	28/5/38
Birkenhead	24/11/45
Brunswick	12/1/57
Birkenhead	1/6/57
Crewe South	28/10/61
*Same date on History Card	

47530 Boilers	
No.10236	16/5/38
No.6200	26/9/42
No.6767	5/2/46
No.6854	4/3/53
No.14118	6/4/60

47531

Built as 16614 at W Beardmore Ltd 13th March 1928
Renumbered 7531 3/4/36; 47531 w/e 3/11/51
19/10/33 Fitting carriage warming gear
19/10/33 Fitting clips to coal slacking pipe
15/5/43 Fitting steel in lieu of copper in boiler tubes
22/5/54 Fitting independent steam brake valves
Withdrawn w/e 11/2/67

47531 Repairs	
7/10/30-17/10/30LS	44,090
12/8/32-25/8/32LS	34,316
2/10/33-19/10/33HG	20,466
12/3/36-3/4/36HS	56,709
29/11/37-11/12/37LO	39,031
24/4/38-20/5/38HS	9,159
5/4/41-7/5/41HG	61,584
23/2/43-26/3/43HS	45,147
28/11/47-2/1/48HG	88,221 Derby
29/9/51-31/10/51LI	77,132 Bow
6/4/54-13/5/54HG	45,056 Bow
27/9/58-16/10/58HI	69,475 Derby
22/5/61-10/8/61HG	31,545 Derby

47531 Sheds	
Carlisle	17/3/28
Mold Jct	31/3/28
Widnes	26/5/28
Willesden	24/4/29
Barrow	14/12/57
Warrington	8/6/63
Carnforth	13/6/64
Workington	14/8/65
Lostock Hall	31/12/66
Stored serviceable	
25/10/64-18/8/65	

47531 Boilers	
No.7513	7/5/41
No.7525	2/1/48
No.7855	13/5/54
No.13975	10/8/61

A smart 47530 at Crewe South, about 1964.

A distinct contrast. Scruffy with the usual coal lumps draping the roof, 47531 is at Kingmoor MPD on 2 October 1966. It is so bedraggled and abandoned as to suggest it's already withdrawn but with Workington 12D plate removed it will be on its way to Lostock Hall for a further couple of months. Doubtless Lostock Hall was delighted with its latest acquisition. A. Scarsbrook, Initial Photographics.

47532

Built as 16615 at W Beardmore Ltd 31st March 1928
Renumbered 7532 15/9/34; 47532 w/e 1/4/50
28/1/39 Manually operated blowdown valves
18/4/42 Fitting steel in lieu of copper boiler tubes
23/4/50 Fitting independent steam brake valves
Withdrawn w/e 30/3/63

47532 Repairs	
18/10/30-1/11/30LS	44,493
4/12/34-24/1/35HG	60,732
4/1/38-20/1/38LS	75,199
12/4/40-25/4/40HG	55,237
28/2/42-17/4/42HS	55,446
21/6/44-14/8/44LS	65,485
1/4/47-28/4/47HG	78,230 Derby
9/3/50-27/3/50HI	82,899 Derby
16/10/53-12/11/53HG	93,635 Derby
19/2/57-6/3/57HI	84,468 Derby
24/1/60-3/3/60HG	73,651 Derby
7/62	? Derby

47532 Sheds	
Dawsholm	31/3/28
Lancaster	6/10/34

47532 Boilers	
No.7879	25/4/40
No.11084	28/4/47
No.11134	12/11/53
No.12683	3/3/60

47534

Built as 16617 at W Beardmore Ltd 31st March 1928
Renumbered 7534 28/1/38; 47534 w/e 30/4/49
19/3/38 Independent steam brake valves
15/6/40 Manually operated blowdown valves
15/6/40 Fitting plate to bunker rails to prevent coal spillage
Withdrawn w/e 25/3/67

47534 Repairs	
10/12/30-27/12/30LS	61,614
17/1/34-3/2/34HG	80,296
13/12/37-31/12/37LS	97,023
18/10/38-15/11/38HS	18,796
3/5/40-25/5/40HG	37,787
1/9/43-23/9/43LS	53,103
13/11/45-5/1/46HG	64,988
29/12/47-29/1/48LS	60,042 Derby
31/3/49-25/4/49LC	34,389 Derby
29/1/51-22/2/51HG	46,808 Derby
26/11/52-15/12/52LC	42,702 Derby
23/11/53-18/12/53HI	22,460 Bow
22/12/53-24/12/53NC	Nil Bow
15/10/54-3/11/54LC	17,917 Derby
15/8/56-31/8/56HG	49,655 Derby
22/2/60-22/3/60LI	93,618 Derby
26/3/62-17/4/62HG	Derby

47534 Sheds	
St Enoch	31/3/28
Polmadie	27/4/35
Leicester	30/9/39
Derby	22/10/60
Westhouses	19/6/65

47534 Boilers	
No.7536	15/11/38
No.6888	25/5/40
No.7869	5/1/46
No.7518	22/2/51
No.13314	31/8/56

47533

Built as 16616 at W Beardmore Ltd 31st March 1928
Renumbered 7533 9/5/36; 47533 w/e 24/4/48
2/12/39 Manually operated blowdown valves
2/11/57 Modified piston for continuous blowdown gear
Withdrawn w/e 26/11/66

47533 Repairs	
1/10/30-11/10/30LS	45,653
10/4/36-9/5/36HG	73,073
4/10/39-21/11/39LS	87,526
16/6/41-15/7/41HG	41,150
26/5/44-10/6/44LS	87,583
14/1/47-1/2/47HG	79,618 Derby
17/3/48-19/4/48LO	33,985 Derby
27/10/49-24/11/49HI	41,000 Derby
7/11/51-14/12/51HG	51,226 Derby
22/3/55-6/4/55LI	68,905 Derby
26/9/57-17/10/57HG	45,093 Derby
15/3/61-3/5/61HG	61,652

47533 Sheds	
Dawsholm	31/3/28
St Enoch	5/9/32
Corkerhill	27/4/35
Leicester	9/9/39
Derby	6/2/60
Nottingham	13/1/62
Rowsley	25/5/63
Derby	2/5/64
Birkenhead	14/6/64

47533 Boilers	
No.7903	15/7/41
No.5483	1/2/47
No.7825	14/12/51
No.13969	17/10/57
No.13627	3/5/61

47534 at Westhouses MPD, where it had arrived in June 1965. It was withdrawn in March 1967 and may well have found itself on the Williamthorpe Colliery 'roster' (see Part One for this episode in the Jinty story). SCOTCHED! presumably refers to its 'scotching' at some previous point; that is, its securing with chocks so it couldn't move – it would have been in steam. It certainly wasn't a warning you could easily miss... RailOnline

47535

Built as 16618 at W Beardmore Ltd 31st March 1928
Renumbered 7535 31/1/38; 47535 w/e 19/3/49
19/3/38 Independent steam brake valves
18/5/46 Manually operated blowdown valves
Withdrawn w/e 22/1/66

47535 Repairs	
20/6/32-2/7/32LS	93,913
29/11/33-16/12/33HG	37,879
12/4/38-7/5/38HS	108,599
10/5/39-20/6/39HG	22,711
12/2/42-21/2/42LS	44,359
11/2/44-19/2/44LO	38,416
18/6/44-18/7/44HS	5,780
21/8/46-20/9/46LS	50,923
22/2/49-15/3/49HG	59,146 Derby
9/4/52-5/5/52HI	60,780 Derby
11/4/55-28/4/55HG	52,514 Derby
16/6/58-7/7/58LI	67,696 Derby
21/11/61-8/12/61HG	- Derby

47535 Sheds	
St Enoch	21/3/28
Polmadie	27/4/35
Widnes	30/9/39
Hasland	20/12/41
Westhouses	17/10/64

47535 Boilers	
No.7538	20/6/39
No.10232	18/7/44
No.13293	15/3/49
No.13301	28/4/55

47536

Built as 16619 at W Beardmore Ltd 31st March 1928
Renumbered 7536 3/5/34; 47536 w/e 26/6/48
3/9/38 Independent steam brake valves
12/8/39 Injector overflow gear removed
7/10/39 Cooling down adaptor
6/9/41 Regulator handle extension
16/6/46 Fitting plate to bunker rails to prevent coal spillage
24/6/48 Fitting copper tubes in lieu of steel boiler tubes
16/7/49 Fitting steel in lieu of copper boiler tubes
Withdrawn w/e 16/6/62

47536 Repairs	
5/9/32-14/9/32LS	93,567
5/4/34-3/5/34HG	38,452
1/9/37-23/9/37HS	82,752
27/5/38-14/6/38HG	14,595
3/5/41-28/5/41LS	69,182
1/11/43-18/11/43HG	51,517
23/1/46-23/2/46LS	52,369
29/5/48-24/6/48HG	54,725 St Rollox
5/4/49-25/4/49LC	18,972 St Rollox
23/3/51-14/4/51HI	- St Rollox
19/5/52-21/5/52LC	- St Rollox
15/5/53-6/6/53HG	- St Rollox
10/2/56-7/3/56LI	- St Rollox
20/7/57-9/8/57HC	- St Rollox
26/3/58-5/4/58HG	- St Rollox

47536 Sheds	
St Enoch	31/3/28
Polmadie	27/4/35
Greenock	23/2/57
Polmadie	2/11/57
Motherwell	27/2/60

47536 Boilers	
No.7542	14/6/38
No.7535	18/11/43
No.6753	24/6/48

47537

Built as 16620 at W Beardmore Ltd 31st March 1928
Renumbered 7537 6/10/34; 47537 w/e 2/4/49
20/11/37 Independent steam brake valves
12/8/39 Injector overflow gear removed
7/10/39 Cooling down adaptor
16/6/46 Fitting plate to bunker rails to prevent coal spillage
19/6/49 Regulator handle extension
17/7/49 Fitting steel tubes in lieu of copper boiler tubes
Withdrawn w/e 20/8/60

47537 Repairs	
24/2/30-28/3/30LO	38,220
14/4/31-2/5/31LS	24,251
13/9/34-3/10/34HG	76,650
29/10/37-23/11/37LS	74,100
28/10/38-15/12/38HS	21,649
30/7/41-23/8/41LS	66,157
31/1/44-12/2/44HG	55,881
23/11/46-12/12/46HS	60,468
23/2/49-28/3/49G	48,389
21/3/51-4/5/51LI	40,874 Kilmarnock
4/6/53-8/8/53G	33,367 St Rollox
2/12/55-7/1/56LI	42,307 St Rollox

47537 Sheds	
St Enoch	31/3/28
Polmadie	27/4/35
Kingmoor	24/11/56

47537 Boilers	
No.7537	15/12/38
No.7542	12/2/44
No.7535	28/3/49
N0.6753	8/8/53

16619 at the cavernous Glasgow St Enoch shed, once of the Glasgow & South Western Railway, which closed in 1935. 16619, as 7536 then 47536, was a rarity amongst Jinties in that it spent its entire working life in Scotland and for overhaul trundled the few miles across the city to the former Caledonian works at St Rollox. It was this existence far from the prying eyes of Derby that later enabled it to run for period with a home-made bunker extension in timber. The planking took its coal carrying capacity right up to the top of the roof. Rail Archive Stephenson.

Another Scottish Jinty, 47537 at Polmadie in the 1950s. Coal on roof as usual, three coal rails. It went to Kingmoor which, though in England, was in fact 'Scottish' in that it stayed in the Scottish Region until 1958. Kingmoor was of course Caledonian in origin. RailOnline

47538

Built as 16621 at W Beardmore Ltd 7th April 1928
Renumbered 7538 3/12/34; 47538 w/e 19/11/49
6/12/34 Fitting light shield for sliding firedoor
31/12/39 Manually operated blowdown valves
3/12/49 Fitting independent steam brake valves
3/12/49 Modification to trailing sand boxes
3/12/49 Regulator handle extension
Withdrawn w/e 13/6/59

47538 Repairs	
18/2/33-17/3/33LS	69,351
27/10/34-6/12/34HG	25,721
4/8/36-22/8/36LO	34,995
27/9/37-2/10/37LO	22,495
7/12/37-22/12/37HS	3,474
28/2/39-7/3/39LO	23,160
7/12/39-20/12/39HS	17,100
19/10/42-14/11/42LS	42,622
27/7/44-10/9/44HG	39,928
24/1/47-1/3/47LS	65.530
24/10/49-15/11/49HG	68,203 Derby
10/1/53-26/1/53LI	57,903 Derby
24/5/56-13/6/56HG	69,740 Derby

47538 Sheds	
Ardrossan	7/4/28
Cricklewood	6/10/34
Kentish Town	21/11/36
Stourton	18/2/39
Ardsley	18/5/58
Wakefield	22/2/59

47538 Boilers	
No.7870	20/12/39
No.12050	10/9/44
No.11555	15/11/49
No.7530	13/6/56

47539

Built as 16622 at W Beardmore Ltd 7th April 1928
Renumbered 7539 16/6/36; 47539 w/e 21/1/50
2/6/38 Independent steam brake valves
3/11/39 Manually operated blowdown valves
Withdrawn w/e 9/2/63

47539 Repairs	
12/12/31-26/12/31LS	55,633
27/7/34-8/10/34HS	40,220
13/5/36-16/6/36LS	33,681
5/5/37-15/5/37LO	19,286
18/5/38-2/6/38HS	22,454
26/9/39-19/10/39HG	34,577
17/9/41-7/10/41LS	52,670
13/4/43-11/5/43LS	46,191
8/2/45-14/3/45HG	52,031
19/8/47-9/947HS	73,183 Derby
28/12/49-19/1/50HG	66,076 Derby
11/4/53-7/5/53HI	86,037 Derby
1/9/56-27/9/56HG	71,927 Derby
18/5/58-4/6/58HG	40,102 Derby

47539 Sheds	
Ardrossan	7/4/28
Kentish Town	6/10/34
Toton	1/1/38
Nottingham	6/8/38
Barnwood	22/5/54
Horton Road	14/7/62
Bath Green Park	6/10/62

47539 Boilers	
No.7869	19/10/39
No.10528	14/3/45
No.8056	19/1/50
No.7502	27/9/56
No.11673	4/6/58

47540

Built as 16623 at W Beardmore Ltd 14th April 1928
Renumbered 7540 18/8/36; 47540 w/e 28/8/48
4/5/34 Fitting carriage warming apparatus
11/6/38 Independent steam brake valves
9/8/41 Regulator handle extension
Withdrawn w/e 15/4/61

47540 Repairs	
4/3/30-24/3/30LS	46,187
8/12/31-23/12/31LS	49,474
4/4/34-4/5/34LS	46,806
25/6/36-18/8/36HG	35,741
26/6/41-8/8/41HG	97,243
18/1/44-12/2/44LS	60,404
21/1/46-18/2/46HG	43,212
22/7/48-28/8/48LS	56,446
20/8/49-2/9/49LC	23,737
1/10/49-3/12/49LC	398
10/5/50-26/5/50LC	8,325
16/4/51-15/5/51HG	17,619 St Rollox
15/6/53-10/7/53HI	43,352 St Rollox
30/9/54-15/10/54LC	20,602 St Rollox
21/10/55-12/11/55G	36,281 St Rollox

47540 Sheds	
Inverness	14/4/28
Forres	28/9/35
Polmadie	9/9/39
Kingmoor	6/6/56

47540 Boilers	
No.7543	8/8/41
No.7537	18/2/46
No.6751	15/5/51
No.7542	12/11/55

A smart 7538, at Cricklewood MPD. It had been renumbered at a Heavy General at the end of 1934, which promptly saw it transferred all the way south from Ardrossan to here.

'Somewhere in Scotland' is about the best that can be managed for this one. 16624 was another Jinty which spent all its time there, next as 7541 then in due course as 47541. Rail Archive Stephenson.

47541

Built as 16624 at W Beardmore Ltd 26th April 1928
Renumbered 7541 23/1/36; 47541 w/e 12/8/50
31/8/32 Fitting carriage warming apparatus
9/8/38 Independent steam brake valves
31/10/42 Regulator handle extension
16/6/46 Fitting plate to bunker handle rails to prevent coal spillage
28/12/47 Removal of sandbox extensions
17/7/49 Fitting steel in lieu of copper boiler tubes
Withdrawn w/e 18/6/60

Repairs		
17/8/32-31/8/32LS	84,934	
22/1/34-9/2/34LS	38,310	
10/12/35-23/1/36HG	54,416	
25/7/38-9/8/38LS	44,690	
2/3/40-29/3/40HS	25,190	
21/8/42-10/10/42HG	51,274	
10/2/45-24/3/45LS	71,526 St Rollox	
8/11/47-4/12/47HG	71,509 St Rollox	
28/6/50-18/8/50LI	73,252	
15/8/51-26/9/51LC	-	Inverness
20/3/53-1/10/53HG	-	St Rollox
30/1/56-18/2/56	-	St Rollox

47541 Sheds	
Inverness	26/4/28
Polmadie	no date
Greenock	9/9/50
Polmadie	25/2/56
Motherwell	27/2/60

47541 Boilers	
No.6753	10/10/42
No.6743	4/12/47

47541 newly renumbered, in the Inverness roundhouse. The '1' at the end is just about squeezed in and the smokebox number plate is yet to arrive, though the new BR 60A plate has been fixed; Furness lubricator still present, in BR days – this was unusual. It was one of the few to be repaired (in BR days at least) at Inverness. Most of these Scottish Jinties went early on – doubtless because of their small numbers. Rail Archive Stephenson.

47542

Built as 16625 at Hunslet Engine Co. 25th November 1927
Renumbered 7542 24/12/35; 47542 w/e 16/9/50
19/4/45 Fitting steel in lieu of copper boiler tubes
7/10/50 Fitting independent steam brake valves
7/10/50 Modifications to trailing sand boxes
Withdrawn w/e 26/5/62

47542 Repairs		
10/12/29-31/12/29LO	45,351	
16/5/30-28/5/30LO	7,779	
30/6/30-15/7/30LS	1,827	
11/10/30-23/10/30LO	59,661	
18/2/31-10/3/31LO	?	
11/8/31-9/9/31HG	?	
12/5/32-24/5/32LO	15,736	
28/12/32-10/2/33LO	10,682	
11/4/33-15/5/33LO	3,908	
2/9/33-15/9/33LO	5,132	
29/10/34-5/11/34LO	26,047	
12/2/35-21/3/35LS	4,853	
27/11/35-31/12/35HG	14,008	
27/9/39-4/10/39LO	63,036	
20/3/40-13/4/40HG	14,739	
29/2/44-20/3/44LS	60,784	
10/4/45-25/4/45HS	16,574	
29/9/48-2/11/48LS	63,634 Bristol	
31/1/49-23/2/49LC	4,769 Shed	
26/7/50-14/9/50HG	23,859 Derby	
12/12/55-4/1/56HG	68,575 Derby	
23/10/59-31/10/59U	-	Bristol

47542 Sheds	
Normanton	14/12/27
Radstock	22/12/34
Bath	15/4/39
Radstock	18/12/43
Templecombe	29/11/58

47542 Boilers	
No.7540	13/4/40
No.7470	25/4/45
No.7874	14/9/50
No.13304	4/1/56

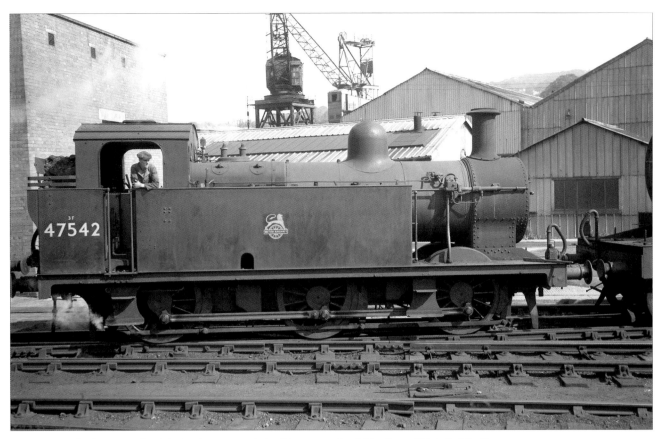

47542 at Bath Green Park MPD in the 1950s; it had been on the S&D since 1934. RailOnline

Jinties could be found the length of the S&D main line – well, at least as far as Templecombe. Behind 47542 stands the distinctive shed building erected by the Southern Region to replace the decrepit S&D structure. Collection Michael Boakes.

47543

Built as 16626 at Hunslet Engine Co. 25th November 1927
Renumbered 7543 8/10/36; 47543 w/e 25/12/48
1/6/33 Fitting clips for coal slacking pipe
27/1/52 Fitting independent steam brake valves
Withdrawn w/e 23/10/65

47543 Repairs	
12/4/29-2/5/29LO	31,094
14/5/29-1/6/29LO	3,411
18/3/30-2/4/30LO	15,654
2/5/30-17/5/30LS	726
15/10/30-4/11/30LO	8,748
20/3/31-24/4/31HG	8,644
6/7/32-27/7/32LO	26,853
7/11/32-28/11/32LO	4,470
1/5/33-1/6/33HS	7,012
19/9/36-8/10/36LS	67,506
7/4/38-11/5/38HG	36,993
1/6/40-17/6/40LS	50,719
4/4/41-22/4/41LS	19,868
17/8/43-17/9/43HG	59,952
16/3/46-10/4/46HS	55,575
20/10/48-24/12/48HG	60,698 Bow
5/12/51-9/1/52LI	62,583 Bow
14/2/55-17/3/55HG	58,829 Bow
8/11/61-16/2/62HG	- Derby

47543 Sheds	
Normanton	14/12/27
Radstock	22/12/34
Bath	no date
Wellingborough	18/4/36
Leicester	6/7/57
Cricklewood	10/3/62
Hasland	3/8/63
Westhouses	17/10/64

47543 Boilers	
No.7554	11/5/38
No.11665	17/9/43
No.7506	24/12/48
No.7507	17/3/55

47544

Built as 16627 at Hunslet Engine Co. 2nd December 1927
Renumbered 7544 13/5/36; 47544 w/e 2/7/49
28/4/31 Fitting clips for coal slacking pipe
10/8/40 Manually operated blowdown valves
10/8/40 Fitting plate to bunker rails to prevent coal spillage
12/7/52 Fitting independent steam brake valves
Withdrawn w/e 27/11/65

47544 Repairs	
10/4/29-7/5/29LO	30,437
14/9/29-29/9/29LO	8,690
19/2/30-1/3/30LO	9,762
10/6/30-24/6/30LO	5,406
8/9/30-20/9/30LS	4,458
6/11/30-14/11/30LO	?
21/5/31-3/6/31LO	72,381
15/10/31-12/11/31HG	6,759
27/3/35-2/5/35LS	70,086
20/4/36-14/5/36HO	16,101
9/11/37-7/12/37HS	28,352
17/7/40-1/8/40HS	46,227
25/7/43-21/8/43HG	47,025
31/8/46-11/10/46LS	65,313 Bristol
7/6/49-1/7/49HG	65,249 Derby
16/6/52-3/7/52LI	72,727 Derby
6/11/54-25/11/54HG	53,830 Derby
24/6/57-8/7/57HI	59,864 Derby
4/9/60-21/10/60HG	65,571 Derby

47544 Sheds	
Normanton	29/11/27
Radstock	22/12/34
Bath	15/4/39
Radstock	20/1/40
Bristol	16/12/44
Bath	24/3/62

47544 Boilers	
No.7864	1/8/40
No.11549	21/8/43
No.13308	1/7/49
N0.14117	25/11/54
No.14073	21/10/60

47543, twenty years a Wellingborough engine, in the yard there on 17 February 1957. K.C.H. Fairey, ColourRail

47544 nearing the level crossing at Radstock from Midsomer Norton after banking a down train on 21 September 1964. The Jinty had come to the S&D a couple of years before and was withdrawn at the end of 1965. At Christmastime it was reported as 'partially dismantled' in the yard at Bath Green Park. ColourRail

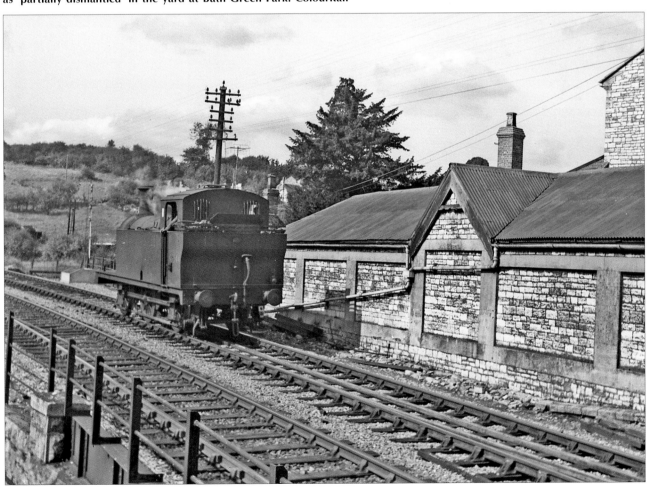

47545

Built as 16628 at Hunslet Engine Co. 10th December 1927
Renumbered 7545 29/4/35; 47545 w/e 8/5/48
16/2/38 Independent steam brake valves
13/7/40 Manually operated blowdown valves
Withdrawn w/e 4/8/62

47545 Repairs	
18/6/29-15/7/29LO	36,917
20/2/30-14/3/30LO	11,543
22/6/30-12/7/30HG	4,976
18/12/30-31/12/30LO	10,389
16/10/31-26/10/31LO	17,363
17/6/32-11/7/32LO	14,499
8/3/33-28/4/33LO	13,857
10/1/34-27/1/34LS	12,881
6/4/35-1/5/35LS	-
29/1/38-16/2/38HS	75,231
8/6/40-20/6/40HS	59,792
30/11/42-23/12/42LS	62,918
3/7/45-2/8/45HG	68,236
5/4/48-5/5/48LS	70,056 Derby
9/2/49-24/2/49LC	17,907 Derby
18/12/51-22/1/52HG	62,618 Derby
16/8/54-2/9/54HI	56,364 Derby
27/9/56-16/10/56HG	53,343 Derby
15/10/60-29/11/60HI	75,257 Derby

47545 Sheds	
Normanton	29/11/27
Sheffield	30/10/33
Saltley	6/11/48
Toton	17/12/49
Nottingham	7/1/50
Toton	18/2/50
Staveley	1/8/53
Stored serviceable 18/9/50-19/3/51	

47545 Boilers	
No.7531	20/6/40
No.10527	2/8/45
No.10582	22/1/52
No.14301	16/10/56

47546

Built as 16629 at Hunslet Engine Co. 17th December 1927
Renumbered 7546 25/5/36; 47546 w/e 26/2/49
8/10/32 Clips for coal slacking pipe
3/9/38 Manually operated blowdown valves
3/9/38 Independent steam brake valves
26/2/40 Regulator handle extension
26/2/40 Modifications to trailing sand boxes
26/2/40 Fitting steel in lieu of copper boiler tubes
7/9/57 Modified pistons for continuous blowdown valves
Withdrawn w/e 7/7/62

47546 Repairs	
29/10/31-26/11/31LS	72,203
20/9/32-8/10/32HG	15,404
14/10/35-25/10/35LS	65,533
2/5/36-26/5/36HO	15,247
24/6/38-25/8/38HG	54,262
24/4/42-13/5/42LS	-
18/12/43-25/1/44HG	155,914
24/9/46-21/10/46HS	72,783 Bow
27/1/49-25/2/49HG	66,440 Derby
28/8/51-12/9/51LI	75,843 Derby
16/8/54-17/9/54HG	82,610 Derby
29/5/57-14/6/57HG	75,035 Derby

47546 Sheds	
Sheffield	29/11/27
Canklow	28/9/35
Leeds	3/4/48
Canklow	22/5/48
Newton Heath	28/2/59

47546 Boilers	
No.10311	25/8/38
No.7469	25/1/44
No.10240	25/2/49
No.7891	17/9/54
No.14208	14/6/57

A fine black Jinty after overhaul with no clue as to location; the only Heavy General for 7545 to merit repainting during its time with this number took place in 1945 and in this picture it may have returned home to Sheffield that year. Rail Archive Stephenson.

And another fine black Jinty after overhaul with no clue as to location! This is probably after its Heavy General of 1952, or even 1956. A few dents have been acquired, duly painted over if not deemed serious. Rail Archive Stephenson.

47547

Built as 16630 at Hunslet Engine Co. 17th December 1927
Renumbered 7547 28/2/36; 47547 w/e 25/9/48
28/1/39 Independent steam brake valves
28/1/39 Manually operated blowdown valves
Withdrawn w/e 7/12/63

47547 Repairs	
9/10/31-23/10/31LS	71,669
9/7/32-23/8/32HO	14,777
20/7/33-25/8/33LS	18,272
9/1/36-28/2/36HG	67,803
19/12/38-4/1/39HS	73,047
27/2/41-28/3/41HG	66,896
29/9/43-21/10/43LS	77,493
10/12/45-18/1/46HG	60,368
17/8/48-22/9/48HS	74,053 Derby
28/6/51-17/7/51HG	78,921 Derby
26/11/53-17/12/53HG	66,972 Derby
13/11/56-30/11/56HG	79,676 Derby

47547 Sheds	
Sheffield	29/11/27
Canklow	28/9/35
Newton Heath	28/2/59

47547 Boilers	
No.6822	28/3/41
No.10586	18/1/46
No.13957	17/7/51
No.10233	30/11/56

47548

Built as 16631 at Hunslet Engine Co. 31st December 1927
Renumbered 7548 27/3/36; 47548 w/e 24/9/49
18/1/33 Fitting clip for coal slacking pipe
4/1/38 Independent steam brake valves
4/1/38 Manually operated blowdown valves
13/7/57 Modified pistons for continuous blowdown valves
Withdrawn w/e 18/8/62

47548 Repairs	
30/7/30-29/8/30LS	45,491
1/1/33-18/1/33HG	85,339
16/3/36-27/3/36LS	?
11/12/37-4/1/38HG	37,236
3/7/39-7/10/39HS	38,235
30/9/41-21/10/41LS	54,009
2/3/44-29/3/44HG	65,615
30/9/46-2/11/46HS	59,907
29/8/49-22/9/49HG	68,165 Derby
5/9/50-9/10/50LC	25,810 Derby
30/10/52-20/11/52LI	81,080 Derby
23/11/54-21/12/54HG	51,933 Derby
12/6/57-26/6/57LI	62,869 Derby
9/10/59-11/11/59HG	36,466 Derby

47548 Sheds	
Sheffield	29/11/27
Cricklewood	11/10/47
Grimesthorpe	17/1/48
Canklow	10/9/61

47548 Boilers	
No.10031	17/12/37
No.11878	29/3/44
No.7903	22/9/49
No.14124	21/12/54
No.14388	11/11/59

47549

Built as 16632 at Hunslet Engine Co. 31st December 1927
Renumbered 7549 31/8/36; carried M prefix; 47549 w/e 25/11/50
30/10/38 Independent steam brake valves
30/10/38 Manually operated blowdown valves
13/7/57 Modified pistons for continuous blowdown valves
Withdrawn w/e 18/7/64

47549 Repairs	
30/3/31-17/4/31LS	54,178
8/6/33-1/8/33HG	41,646
29/9/34-2/10/34LO	31,863
21/2/36-2/3/36LO	38,285
27/7/36-31/8/36HS	9,717
19/4/38-25/4/38LO	39,900
2/8/38-29/10/38HG	6,495
8/5/41-22/5/41LS	67,661
24/6/43-30/7/43HG	63,154
30/10/45-12/12/45LS	70,617
12/3/48-2/4/48HG	63,881 Derby
16/10/50-23/11/50HI	69,130 Bow
25/10/54-17/11/54HG	99,856 Derby
3/6/57-12/7/57HG	64,312 Bow
20/6/61-6/7/61HI	94,144 Derby

47549 Sheds	
Nottingham	29/11/27
Bedford	2/12/46
Horwich Works	25/5/63

47549 Boilers	
No.7560	29/10/38
No.11551	30/7/43
No.7545	2/4/48
No.13730	17/11/54
No.14206	12/7/57

7548 at Sheffield Grimesthorpe MPD, from where it worked for many years. It was renumbered in April 1949 and 47513 behind had been similarly dealt with in June 1948, so this is the period we are looking at. The engines appear to be on one of the radiating stalls off the outside turntable, installed in anticipation of the construction of a second roundhouse, which never materialised. RailOnline

7549 at Bedford about 1949. It certainly stood out for a while when BR came into existence, acquiring (one of only three to do so) the M prefix. The BRITISH RAILWAYS is in large 10 inch lettering in a kind of mixed Gill sans/block style.

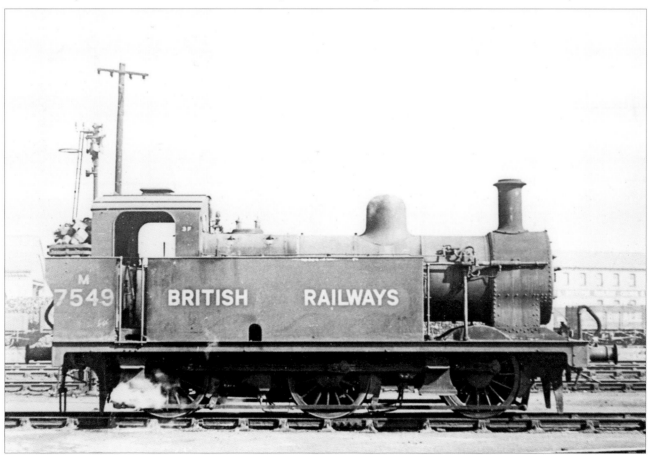

47550

Built as 16633 at Hunslet Engine Co. 3rd January 1928
Renumbered 7550 9/1/35; 47550 w/e 6/10/51
9/1/32 Fitting clips for coal slacking pipe
18/6/36 Fitting light shields for sliding firedoors
6/9/41 Manually operated blowdown valves
2/11/46 Fitting steel in lieu of copper boiler tubes
2/11/46 Modification to trailing sand boxes
3/11/51 Fitting independent steam brake valves
Withdrawn w/d 14/3/64

47550 Repairs	
31/7/30-8/8/30LS	66,439
20/12/31-9/1/32HG	29,593
22/11/34-10/1/35LS	72,419
27/4/36-18/6/36HG	32,284
4/2/39-16/2/39LO	66,891
25/4/39-27/6/39LS	4,529
11/8/41-1/9/41HG	52,423
27/2/43-27/3/43LS	44,764
20/9/46-25/10/46HG	77,879 Derby
25/7/49-13/8/49LI	60,212 Bristol
21/8/51-5/10/51HG	50,023 Derby
25/10/54-8/11/54LI	70,984 Derby
16/3/57-4/4/57HG	53,340 Derby
12/62	? Horwich

47550 Sheds	
Nottingham	1/1929
Bristol	31/7/43
Bank Hall	28/3/59
Horwich Works	13/1/62

47550 Boilers	
No.6755	1/9/41
No.7613	25/10/46
No.13969	5/10/51
No.14308	4/4/57

47551

Built as 16634 at Hunslet Engine Co. 19th January 1928
Renumbered 7551 20/1/36; 47551 w/e 10/7/48
8/4/33 Fitting clips for coal slacking pipe
24/6/38 Manually operated blowdown valves
28/1/50 Fitting independent steam brake valves
Withdrawn w/e 23/2/63

47551 Repairs	
6/8/30-13/8/30LS	58,170
25/3/33-8/4/33HG	58,784
1/1/36-20/1/36LS	67,948
12/10/37-20/10/37LO	43,355
23/2/38-24/6/38HG	9,084
23/10/40-4/11/40LS	64,056
28/6/44-19/7/44HG	95,183
11/3/47-19/4/47LS	78,072 Leeds
16/6/48-8/7/48LO	32,735 Derby
24/2/49-4/3/49LC	49,289 Shed
21/12/49-13/1/50HG	21,423
30/1/56-22/2/56HG	92,713 Derby
6/3/56-7/3/56NC(rect)	783 Derby

47551 Sheds	
Nottingham	1/1929
Toton	6/8/38

47551 Boilers	
No.10308	25/3/38
No.6669	19/7/44
No.13320	13/1/50
No.13293	22/2/56

47550 at Bristol Barrow Road MPD in the late 1950s. It ended up as one of the Horwich works shunters. RailOnline

47551, ever-present at Toton since before the War, inside the shed in the 1960s. The problem of housing the giant Garratts had been solved by taking a long straight road through roundhouses No.1 and No.2 and there it is, complete with continuous smoke vent, resulting in the foreshortening of a number of turntable stalls – suited to Jinties, it is clear. With the Garratts gone, the long road proved useful for the examination of DMUs – crucially, under cover. It was perhaps the most unusual of all BR's primitive ad hoc reactions to the new, unfamiliar art of diesel servicing. In 1950 there were thirty or so Jinties at Toton but even there they were not strictly shunters, by any means. The hump shunting was done by about fifteen diesel shunters, with their more useful gear ratios for slow speed, high power working. RailOnline

47552

Built as 16635 at Hunslet Engine Co. 19th January 1928
Renumbered 7552 2/11/36; 47552 w/e 29/10/49
3/11/36 Fitting protector plates for vacuum stand pipes
3/11/36 Independent steam brake valves
13/6/42 Manually operated blowdown valves
Withdrawn w/e 17/11/62

47552 Repairs	
19/2/30-27/2/30LS	59,259
2/10/32-14/10/32LS	53,918
24/8/33-15/9/33HG	20,438
17/10/36-3/11/36HS	77,634
14/10/39-28/10/39LS	73,488
12/5/42-4/6/42HG	66,021
26/7/44-17/8/44HS	62,949
21/4/47-16/5/47HG	77,305 Derby
26/9/49-24/10/49LI	71,378 Derby
22/4/52-22/5/52HG	71,019 Derby
24/11/53-2/12/53LC	33,875 Shed
29/9/55-19/10/55LI	41,957 Derby
13/6/58-31/7/58HG	60,833 Derby

47552 Sheds	
Nottingham	1/1929
Bristol	10/1/53
Templecombe	31/10/59
Bristol	30/1/60
Templecombe	19/5/62

47552 Boilers	
No.6851	4/6/42
No.7887	16/5/47
No.13986	22/5/52
No.6833	31/7/58

47552 in its previous manifestation as 7552; the year could well be 1947, after a Heavy General.

Above and below. Suitably enough in slightly ghostly images, 16636 and then as 7553, the Jinty which was re-gauged in 1944 and sold (along with 7456) to the Northern Counties Committee to see out its days in Ulster – see *The Emerald Isle* in Part One.

47554

Built as 16637 at Hunslet Engine Co. 30th January 1928
Renumbered 7554 31/1/36; 47554 w/e 17/12/49
16/1/33 Fitting clips for coal slacking pipe
10/9/36 Fitting light shields for sliding fire doors
10/9/36 Independent steam brake valve
2/12/39 Manually operated blowdown valves
Withdrawn w/e 25/8/62

47554 Repairs	
8/5/30-29/5/30LO	47,354
18/12/32-6/1/33HG	44,477
16/1/36-3/1/36LS	66,451
11/7/36-10/9/36HO	9,314
13/9/37-1/10/37HS	25,299
16/10/39-17/11/39HG	50,979
15/6/42-4/7/42LS	70,788
3/11/44-1/12/44HG	51,521
20/6/47-14/7/47LS	59,658 Bow
27/7/49-16/8/49LC	47,443 Shed
21/11/49-16/12/49HG	5,777 Derby
11/6/53-3/7/53LI	73,035 Bow
18/5/56-29/6/56HG	45,897 Bow
15/9/58-21/11/58NC	48,992 Bow
22/7/59-29/9/59LI	17,259 Bow

47554 Sheds	
Wellingborough	1/1929
Kettering	11/7/31
Wellingborough	28/9/35
St Albans	23/10/54
Cricklewood	16/1/60
Kentish Town	15/7/61
Gorton	21/7/62

47554 Boilers	
No.7492	17/11/39
No.10525	1/12/44
No.13314	16/12/49
No.14295	29/6/56

47556

Built as 16639 at Hunslet Engine Co 9th February 1928
Renumbered 7556 20/11/36; 47556 w/e 31/12/49
31/12/49 Modification to trailing sand boxes
31/12/49 Fitting independent steam brake valves
Withdrawn w/e 15/12/62

47556 Repairs	
4/11/31-14/11/31LS	55,104
31/8/33-16/10/33HG	48,174
30/10/36-20/11/36LS	88,378
17/10/38-17/11/38HG	44,926
14/2/42-28/2/42HS	78,041
2/8/44-31/8/44HG	55,106
16/10/46-9/11/46LO	46,764 Shed
27/1/48-11/3/48LS	29,789 Leeds
25/11/49-28/12/49HG	41,326 Derby
10/11/52-22/12/52HG	67,394 Derby
24/11/54-6/1/55HI	42,953 Derby
26/7/58-19/8/58HG	75,090 Derby

47556 Sheds	
Carlisle (Kingmoor, pres.)	1/1929
Carlisle Upperby	22/2/36
Huddersfield	10/12/55
Manningham	9/2/58
York	25/1/59

47556 Boilers	
No.7847	17/11/38
No.5833	31/8/44
No.12050	28/12/49
No.6631	22/12/52
No.13984	19/8/58

47555

Built as 16638 at Hunslet Engine Co. 9th February 1928
Renumbered 7555 5/5/36; 47555 w/e 3/3/51
21/8/37 Protector plates for vacuum stand pipe
21/8/37 Continuous blowdown apparatus
21/8/37 Independent steam brake valves
18/9/42 Fitting steel in lieu of copper boiler tubes
21/4/51 Fitting ATC gear
7/9/57 Modified pistons for continuous blowdown gear
Withdrawn w/e 23/6/62

47555 Repairs	
26/11/31-30/12/31LS	59,792
21/8/33-9/9/33HG	35,081
6/4/36-5/5/36LS	71,147
13/7/37-21/8/37HG	33,974
25/1/40-14/2/40LS	63,517
21/8/42-18/9/42HG	73,145
26/2/45-24/3/45LS	73,410
21/7/47-25/8/47HG	62,464 Derby
18/4/50-26/5/50LI	72,497 Leeds
10/2/51-27/2/51NC	6,920 Bow
29/12/51-5/1/52LC	23,051 Bow
4/11/52-27/11/52LC	16,406
29/1/53-12/2/53NC	- Bow
21/6/54-16/7/54HG	- Bow
23/12/54-9/1/55LC	- Shed
24/5/55-3/6/55LC	18,512 Shed
16/5/56-26/5/56LC	33,684 Shed
12/7/57-29/8/57HG	18,624
18/9/58-3/10/58LC	22,901 Shed
3/11/59-22/11/59LC	36,601 Plaistow

47555 Sheds	
Carlisle	1/1929
Leeds	30/1/32
Toton	30/10/33
Plaistow	3/3/51
Tilbury	31/10/59
Stored serviceable 18/9/50-9/2/51	

47555 Boilers	
No.10029	13/8/37
No.7904	18/9/42
No.12679	25/8/47
No.7852	16/7/54
No.13623	29/8/57

47555 at Plaistow about 1959; it has mysteriously mislaid its smokebox number plate. 47555 had its moment in the sun 31 October 1958 when the failure of a 2-6-4T saw the Jinty ride to the rescue of the 2.29 Tilbury-Dagenham Dock passenger train. Even more remarkably, the day before following a similar failure, 47512 had taken over an afternoon off-peak Southend train at Barking, taking it into Fenchurch Street. RailOnline

By virtue of passing to the North Eastern Region with its then home shed Huddersfield, 47556 eventually found itself at York; on 30 August 1959 it was stabled among the more or less deserted half ruins of the NER roundhouses south of the station. R.J. Buckley, Initial Photographics.

47557

Built as 16640 at Hunslet Engine Co. 28th February 1928
Renumbered 7557 13/12/34; 47557 w/e 4/2/50
8/10/32 Fitting 'Memno' grease cups
17/12/34 Fitting light shield for sliding firedoor
16/3/38 Independent steam brake valves
28/1/39 Manually operated blowdown valves
14/6/47 Modification to trailing sand boxes
14/6/47 Fitting steel in lieu of copper boiler tubes
Withdrawn w/e 14/2/64

47557 Repairs		
29/4/29-30/5/29HG	22,720	
22/9/29-6/10/29HO	6,401	
9/11/32-15/11/32LS	61,125	
21/11/34-17/12/34HG	47,642	
22/2/38-16/3/38HS	78,568	
5/9/40-24/9/40HG	63,247	
29/7/43-13/8/43LS	65,695	
6/1/44-16/1/44LO	6,806	
19/2/45-28/2/45LO	19,162	
7/5/47-23/5/47HG	34,962	Derby
14/1/50-2/2/50HI	49,804	Derby
27/7/53-10/9/53HG	44,788	Derby
29/1/58-14/2/58HG	58,991	Derby
1/11/60-19/11/60U	-	Bristol
10/3/61-30/3/61U	-	Bristol
23/9/61-20/10/61U	-	Bristol
15/2/63-25/5/63U	-	Bristol

47557 Sheds	
Mold Jct	3/3/28
Worcester	30/9/28
Birmingham	28/9/35
Gloucester	17/12/38
Radstock	21/3/42

47557 Boilers	
No.7496	24/9/40
No.7879	23/5/47
No.7904	10/9/53
No.14322	14/2/58

47558

Built as 16641 at Hunslet Engine Co. 28th February 1928
Renumbered 7558 21/8/36; 47558 w/e 15/10/49
1/3/33 Fitting clips for coal slacking pipe
6/9/36 Screw reversing gear
6/9/36 Fitting destination board brackets
20/4/40 Fitting Wakefield patent fountain type lubricator
Withdrawn w/e 21/3/64

47558 Repairs		
11/8/31-3/9/31LS	60,176	
9/4/32-19/4/32LO	13,469	
8/2/33-1/3/33HG	18,426	
13/11/34-29/11/34LO	45,926	
4/10/35-18/10/35LS	19,958	
28/10/36-12/11/36LO	24,344	
19/3/37-28/4/37HG	8,765	
6/9/38-21/9/38LS	33,494	
8/9/39-20/9/39LO	22,351	
23/2/40-4/4/40HS	9,370	
5/5/41-15/5/41LO	18,838	
5/2/42-16/2/42LS	12,965	
13/2/43-20/2/43LO	17,211	
11/2/44-18/2/44LO	18,207	
31/7/44-24/9/44HG	7,093	
2/11/45-12/11/45LO	17,003	
13/9/46-4/11/46HS	13,741	Bow
15/12/47-27/12/47LO	18,395	Shed
3/12/48-20/12/48LC	16,070	Shed
20/1/49-11/2/49NC	1,484	Bow
14/9/49-11/10/49HI	11,055	Bow
23/9/50-12/10/50LC	16,654	Shed
15/6/51-12/7/51HG	28,644	Derby
18/4/55-11/5/55LI	56,184	Bow
14/1/57-8/3/57HG	24,213	Bow

47558 Sheds	
Mold Jct	3/3/28
Devons Road	20/3/29
Leicester	7/10/29
Devons Road	9/12/39
Bangor	9/11/57
Llandudno Jct	7/11/59
Stored serviceable 25/9/39-4/10/39	

47558 Boilers	
No.5815	4/4/40
No.6871	24/9/44
No.7480	4/11/46
No.7810	12/7/51
No.14305	8/3/57

Radstock's 47557 in a busy scene at Bath Green Park on 1 March 1961; framing the Jinty are an S&D 2-8-0 and one of the line's 4F 0-6-0s. M. Burch, Michael Boakes Collection.

47558 at Devons Road Bow on 16 June 1957, shortly before ejection by diesels. Michael Boakes Collection.

Llandudno Junction's 47558 sorting wagons at the station about 1961; the place was a staging point for traffic from the west of Llandudno destined for Chester and destinations east thereof.

47559

Built as 16642 at Hunslet Engine Co. 14th March 1928
Renumbered 7559 22/5/36; 47559 w/e 31/7/48
20/3/29 Carriage warming gear
6/9/36 Fitting clips for coal slacking pipe
31/12/39 Fitting Wakefield patent fountain type lubricator#
3/7/41 Fitting steel in lieu of copper boiler tubes
Withdrawn w/e 6/5/61

47559 Repairs	
22/1/31-5/2/31LO	53,630
18/3/31-1/4/31LS	2,364
22/3/33-8/4/33HG	36,853
7/3/35-14/3/35LO	47,818
25/10/35-12/11/35LS	14,992
4/5/36-22/5/36LO	9,636
24/4/37-29/5/37HG	18,795
16/4/38-26/4/38LO	25,964
2/6/38-16/6/38LS	2,654
10/4/39-19/4/39LO	18,901
25/11/39-9/12/39LS	13,982
14/4/40-23/4/40LO	8,312
13/6/41-3/7/41HS	17,702
3/6/42-10/6/42LO	16,740
3/6/43-12/6/43LO	18,917
6/9/43-21/9/43LS	4,435
6/6/44-13/6/44LO	15,327
21/8/45-23/10/45HG	22,398
21/10/46-4/11/46LO	18,034 Shed
11/10/47-28/10/47LO	16,19 Bow
21/5/51-13/7/51HG	33,598 Bow
22/3/54-15/4/54HG	38,862 Derby
18/5/54NC	920 Bow
11/2/58-7/3/58HI	56,476 Bow

47559 Sheds	
Crewe Works	17/3/28
'to Mold'	No date
Devons Road	20/3/29
Barrow	23/11/57
Willesden	14/12/57

47559 Boilers	
No.6673	17/5/37
No.6882	3/7/41
No.10239	23/10/45
No.13649	13/7/51
No.14058	15/4/54

47560

Built as 16643 at Hunslet Engine Co. 14th March 1928
Renumbered 7560 4/9/36; 47560 w/e 15/1/49
Modifications and Improvements
6/9/36 Fitting destination board brackets
6/9/36 Fitting screw reversing gear
28/7/37 Continuous blowdown apparatus
28/7/37 Dust shields to trailing axleboxes
Withdrawn w/e 16/7/60

47560 Repairs	
11/9/31-25/9/31LS	65,738
31/1/33-16/2/33HG	25,048
2/7/34-17/7/34LO	36,996
1/7/35-22/7/35LO	21,760
6/11/35-19/11/35LS	6,321
16/11/36-26/11/36LO	22,352
24/6/37-28/7/37HG	11,417
20/6/38-29/6/38LO	26,412
29/9/38-14/10/38HS	7,109
14/6/39-21/6/39LO	15,161
17/2/40-27/2/40LO	14,859
22/5/40-1/6/40LS	5,166
8/3/41-24/3/41LO	12,493
3/3/42-13/3/42LO	17,225
16/7/42-12/9/42HG	6,904
6/9/43-13/9/43LO	20,213
13/9/44-29/9/44LS	18,886
26/11/45-3/12/45LO	21,463
20/11/46-6/12/46LO	16,660 Shed
26/3/47-21/5/47HS	5,312 Bow
31/7/48-25/8/48LO	23,729 Shed
10/12/48-13/1/49HI	5,117 Bow
19/9/50-5/10/50LC	29,211 Bow
1/11/50-22/11/50NC	1,237 Bow
6/2/51-16/3/51HI	3,431 Bow
14/4/53-19/6/53HG	36,910 Derby
23/3/57-18/4/57LI	57,370 Bow

47560 Sheds	
Mold Jct	17/3/28
Devons Road	10/4/29
Speke Jct	26/10/57

47560 Boilers	
No.6870	14/7/37
No.6859	12/9/42
No.6627	21/5/47
No.12687	19/6/53

47561

Built as 16644 at Hunslet Engine Co. 13th April 1928
Renumbered 7561 30/11/35; 47561 w/e 23/7/49
20/3/29 Carriage warming gear
4/10/36 Screw reversing gear
4/10/36 Destination board brackets
8/4/37 Light shields for sliding firedoors
31/12/39 Fitting Wakefield patent fountain type lubricator
Withdrawn w/e 20/8/60

47561 Repairs	
11/2/31-4/3/31LS	47,302
7/10/31-15/10/31LO	10,537
4/12/32-19/12/32HG	22,707
20/6/34-28/6/34LO	37,012
29/9/34-17/10/34LO	7,425
23/8/35-6/9/35LO	16,298
8/11/35-22/11/35LS	5,409
16/6/36-24/6/36LO	13,804
2/3/37-8/4/37HG	17,440
4/4/38-14/4/38LO	27,657
20/5/38-2/6/38HS	1,912
4/4/39-11/4/39LO	19,344
16/12/39-23/12/39HS	15,516
4/4/40-12/4/40LO	5,640
9/5/41-23/5/41LO	23,668
17/5/42-13/6/42HG	18,825
17/5/43-24/5/43LO	17,731
7/7/44-22/7/44LS	20,796
23/10/46-14/12/46HS	40,548 Derby
29/1/48-5/2/48LO	16,448 Shed
31/1/49-8/2/49LC	18,245 Shed
27/6/49-20/7/49HI	5,985 Bow
16/7/50-29/7/50LC	16,498 Shed
26/1/51-13/3/51HG	8,660 Derby
21/1/55-25/2/55HI	57,596 Bow
23/3/57-3/5/57HG	31,088 Bow
31/10/58-11/12/58LC	28,400 Derby

47561 Sheds	
Crewe	21/4/28
Devons Road	19/5/28
Nottingham	16/6/45
Plaistow	6/10/45
Devons Road	23/3/46
Monument Lane	19/10/57

47561 Boilers	
No.7876	13/6/42
No.6871	14/12/46
No.6856	13/3/51
No.14311	3/5/57

47562

Built as 16645 at Hunslet Engine Co. 13th April 1928
Renumbered 7562 29/6/35; 47562 w/e 19/11/49
16/12/36 Carriage warming gear
16/12/36 Fitting screw reversing gear
16/12/36 Fitting destination board brackets
23/3/40 Fitting Wakefield patent fountain type lubricator
23/3/40 manually operated blowdown valves
Withdrawn w/e 1/12/62

47562 Repairs	
19/11/30-10/12/30LS	45,412
28/9/31-7/10/31LO	14,697
26/7/32-10/8/32LO	16,001
9/11/32-22/11/32LS	4,761
27/7/33-23/8/33HO	12,373
25/5/34-8/6/34LO	18,262
4/6/35-29/6/35HG	26,776
27/5/36-4/6/36LO	25,254
2/12/36-16/12/36LS	10,147
15/12/37-24/12/37LO	23,623
26/2/38-11/3/38HS	3,906
14/11/38-24/11/38LO	15,938
30/10/39-9/11/39LO	19,869
28/2/40-16/3/40HS	6,792
16/4/41-1/5/41LO	19,254
13/2/42-27/2/42LS	13,987
5/2/43-13/2/43LO	19,021
4/4/44-28/4/44HG	21,203
19/6/45-28/6/45LO	18,467
17/7/46-28/7/46LO	17,461
13/5/47-11/6/47LO	13,749 Shed
14/1/48-1/3/48HS	11,179 Bow
8/10/49-15/11/49HG	36,144 Derby
13/10/52-3/11/52LI	68,463 Derby
7/10/53-2/11/53LC	21,850 Derby
15/10/56-1/11/56HG	61,980 Derby
1/11/57-21/11/57LC	18,021 Derby

47562 Sheds	
Crewe	21/4/28
Devons Road	19/5/28
Skipton	29/1/49
Accrington	14/12/57
Rose Grove	4/3/61

47562 Boilers	
No.6861	16/3/40
No.11880	28/4/44
No.10233	15/11/49
No.13636	1/11/56

47563

Built as 16646 at Hunslet Engine Co. 26th April 1928
Renumbered 7563 23/9/36; 47563 w/e 3/6/50
20/8/36 Fitting destination board brackets
20/8/36 Fitting screw reversing gear
3/11/39 Fitting Wakefield patent fountain type lubricator
Withdrawn w/e 19/3/60

47563 Repairs	
16/3/31-31/3/31LS	47,090
24/3/32-8/4/32LO	18,167
1/9/32-28/9/32HS	7,103
22/7/35-21/8/35LS	62,260
6/8/36-20/8/36LO	24,721
5/2/37-5/3/37HG	11,280
4/3/38-18/3/38LS	30,433
6/3/39-15/3/39LO	23,778
2/10/39-11/10/39LS	13,314
3/4/40-11/4/40LO	10,324
27/3/41-10/4/41LO	16,609
21/11/41-20/12/41HG	9,869
25/11/42-7/12/42LO	18,289
22/11/43-11/12/43LS	17,314
16/12/44-1/1/45LO	17,531
4/10/45-20/10/45HS	12,270
31/10/46-18/11/46LO	17,395 shed
14/5/47-28/7/47LO	8,280 Bow
20/12/47-29/1/48HS	7,459 Derby
15/5/50-29/5/50LI	55,255 Derby
27/4/53-26/5/53HG	70,624 Derby
7/11/55-17/11/55HI	60,426 Derby

47563 Sheds	
Crewe	28/3/28
Devons Road	19/5/28
Nottingham	29/1/49
Grimesthorpe	18/2/50
Millhouses	30/4/55
Derby	2/6/56
Stored unserviceable 14/2/59-17/3/60	

47563 Boilers	
No.7484	20/12/41
No.7907	29/1/48
No.14044	26/5/53

47564

Built as 16647 at Hunslet Engine Co. 26th April 1928
Renumbered 7564 30/10/36; 47564 w/e 31/7/48
30/10/36 Fitting destination board brackets
30/10/36 Fitting screw reversing gear
2/12/39 Fitting Wakefield patent fountain type lubricator
14/6/41 Manually operated blowdown valves
Withdrawn w/e 20/3/65

47564 Repairs	
9/12/30-6/1/31LS	-
10/11/31-20/11/31LO	55,393
13/10/32-26/10/32LS	33,161?
21/7/33-29/8/33HO	14,306
11/6/34-21/6/34LO	20,282
14/5/35-29/5/35LS	20,512
29/5/36-9/6/36LO	24,188
19/9/36-30/10/36HG	5,650
1/9/37-11/9/37LO	-
28/4/38-12/5/38LS	42,790
26/5/39-3/6/39LO	25,207
4/11/39-11/11/39HS	9,408
6/6/40-15/6/40LO	12,778
26/3/41-17/5/41HG	11,897
29/3/42-8/4/42LO	16,920
6/5/43-14/5/43LS	17,736
29/5/44-5/6/44LO	22,290
26/2/45-23/3/45HS	12,014
12/4/46-25/4/46LO	17,826
3/10/46-20/1/46HS	7,259 Bow
25/12/47-15/1/48LO	19,810 Shed
12/7/48-30/7/48NC	7,182 Bow
17/2/49-1/3/49LC	- Shed
22/6/49-12/7/49HI	5,357 Bow
18/1/51-2/2/51NC	27,381 Bow
14/8/51-1/9/51LCEO	11,066 Shed
13/9/52-17/10/52HG	15,690 Bow
3/11/55-2/12/55LI	45,722 Bow
6/12/55-9/12/55NCrect	- Bow
22/9/59-14/10/59HG	52,916 Derby

47564 Sheds	
Crewe	28/4/28
Devons Road	19/5/28
Barrow	23/4/57
Workington	18/8/62
Barrow	1/9/62
Lostock Hall	11/5/63

47564 Boilers	
No.5949	17/5/41
No.6555	20/11/46
No.7846	17/10/52
No.14383	16/10/59

Pilot work for Lostock Hall's 47564 at Preston, about 1964. Michael Boakes Collection.

Newly overhauled and renumbered 47565 at Derby MPD at the end of 1948; it's probably been brought over from the works by that scruffy half cab 1F tank. Period style, with small lettering and larger numbers; it had been a Lickey banker for some years and remained on the job for another decade.

47565

Built as 16648 at Hunslet Engine Co. 8th May 1928
Renumbered 7565 2/12/35; 47565 w/e 13/11/48
4/10/36 Fitting screw reversing gear
4/10/36 Fitting destination board brackets
16/7/37 Fitting dust shields for trailing axleboxes
Withdrawn w/e 2/4/66

47565 Repairs	
11/3/31-26/3/31LS	49,006
17/8/32-30/8/32LS	-
7/6/33-23/6/33HO	-
12/11/34-28/11/34LS	35,556
13/11/35-4/12/35LO	25,349
7/10/36-16/10/36LO	19,003
19/6/37-16/7/37HG	16,197
11/6/38-18/6/38LO	27,098
26/8/38-9/9/38LS	6,658
6/6/39-15/6/39LO	21,275
29/11/39-12/12/39LS	21,275
23/6/40-29/6/40LO	12,008
29/10/41-15/11/41HG	22,815
1/1/43-19/1/43HS	26,216
5/1/44-1/2/44LO	23,739
14/11/44-29/11/44HS	16,150
19/11/46-21/12/46LS	38,282 Leeds
17/9/47-16/10/47LO	13,850 Derby
18/10/48-10/11/48HG	21,996 Derby
21/2/50-20/3/50HG	26,240 Derby
4/10/51-25/10/51HG	30,890 Derby
12/11/53-11/12/53HG	34,769 Derby
18/4/55-3/5/55HG	27,403 Derby
6/10/56-25/10/56HG	25,481 Derby
30/1/62-23/2/62HG	Derby

47565 Sheds	
Crewe	10/5/28
Devons Road	19/5/28
Gloucester	26/4/41
Bromsgrove	13/9/41
Bidston	14/9/57
Birkenhead	22/11/58
Crewe South	26/12/64
Stored serviceable 25/2/57-12/8/57	

47565 Boilers	
No.6866	6/7/37
No.7515	15/11/41
No.6199	19/1/43
No.11671	29/11/44
No.10241	10/11/48
No.6861	20/3/50
No.13975	25/10/51
No.6770	11/12/53
No.13299	3/5/55
No.7482	25/10/56

47566

Built as 16649 at Hunslet Engine Co. 8th May 1928
Renumbered 7566 11/11/36; 47566 w/e 10/12/49
11/11/36 Fitting destination board brackets
11/11/36 Fitting screw reversing gear
23/3/40 Manually operated blowdown valves
31/12/49 Fitting Wakefield patent fountain type lubricator
5/10/57 Modified pistons for continuous blow down valves
Withdrawn w/e 5/11/66

47566 Repairs	
24/7/30-15/8/30LS	38,694
24/6/31-4/7/31LO	18,704
7/12/31-18/12/31LO	8,237
5/1/33-1/2/33HG	20,456
5/2/35-28/2/35LO	45,314
16/10/35-29/10/35LS	15,241
15/9/36-11/11/36HS	21,311
19/10/37-27/10/37LO	25,948
16/6/38-27/6/38LS	17,657
14/6/39-23/6/39LO	22,488
7/1/40-28/2/40HG	13,596
1/5/41-13/5/41LO	19,699
4/2/42-14/2/42LS	12,606
12/6/44-19/6/44LO	50,188
19/10/44-3/11/44HS	9,934
2/11/46-22/11/46LO	41,733 Shed
14/3/48-8/4/48LS	31,357 Derby
31/10/49-7/12/49HG	30,305 Bow
11/12/54-10/1/55HG	91,761 Derby
9/9/57-26/9/57LI	57,364 Derby
5/1/61-17/2/61HG	77,834 Derby

47566 Sheds	
Crewe	10/5/28
Devons Road	19/5/28
Peterborough	23/1/43
Brunswick	28/3/53
Edge Hill	13/10/56
Aintree	4/7/64
Stored serviceable 16/7/38-26/7/38 30/7/38-3/10/38 20/9/65-27/9/65	

47566 Boilers	
No.6786	28/2/40
No.7864	3/11/44
No.6815	7/12/49
No.6837	10/1/55
No.12687	17/2/61

After years on the Lickey, 47565 entered on the usual peripatetic last few years, in its case here and there in the North West. It finished up here, at Crewe South. RailOnline

7566 running towards Peterborough on the Midland lines from Stamford, hauling a pick-up goods (Class K) about 1949. It's just passed through Walton station, just south of Werrington Junction where the line to Spalding left the East Coast main line (now a burrowing junction). The station served the Midland lines only (as did the next one north, at Helpston) there being no platforms on the ex-GN main lines. The stations closed long before Beeching. Tony Wright continues: 'The train is interesting, mainly (at least at the front) composed of wooden-bodied RCH wagons, probably some ex-PO, with a single all steel one present. Modellers who strive to make their wagons run in a uniform fashion might well copy the real things, with uneven springs giving lop-sided appearances. It's probably a daily working, though where it started is anyone's guess. Melton Mowbray? Oakham? Maybe even just Stamford? No doubt it'll end up somewhere (after a bit of to-ing and fro-ing) in New England Yard, though there were Midland sidings to the West of Peterborough North station. Note the TPO apparatus on the main line on the down side, and the fog hut tilted over to prevent rot from rain getting in. Also, lower-quadrant MR signals on the Stamford line and more modern upper-quadrants on the main line.' RailOnline

47567

Built as 16650 at Hunslet Engine Co. 5th September 1928
Renumbered 7567 4/5/34; 47567 w/e 4/9/48
4/9/43 Regulator handle extension
24/9/43 Fitting steel in lieu of copper boiler tubes
Withdrawn w/e 15/10/60

47567 Repairs	
1/12/30-13/12/30LS	63,510
5/1/33-19/1/33LS	53,996
26/3/34-4/5/34HG	31,695
29/12/36-27/1/37HS	58,506
4/5/39-8/8/39HG	49,741
16/2/42-5/3/42HS	59,555
29/7/43-17/8/43HS	31,557
10/12/45-3/1/46HS	54,166
5/8/48-4/9/48HG	51,081 Derby
12/2/51-14/3/51LI	50,831 Derby
31/8/53-29/9/53HG	49,937 Derby
22/8/56-6/9/56LI	55,554 Derby
7/10/60	Crewe

47567 Sheds	
Low Moor	5/9/28
Farnley Jct	12/12/30
Wakefield	25/1/59

47567 Boilers	
No.7830	8/8/39
No.7522	17/8/43
No.6829	4/9/48
No.6841	29/9/53

47568

Built as 16651 at Hunslet Engine Co. 10th September 1928
Renumbered 7568 17/5/34; 47568 w/e 1/10/49
7/9/57 Modified pistons for continuous blowdown gear
Withdrawn w/e 12/11/60

47568 Repairs	
1/12/30-20/12/30LS	56,169
2/2/33-18/2/33LS	42,498
29/3/34-17/5/34HG	25,614
2/8/37-24/8/37HS	73,713
24/3/38-17/6/38LO	12,622
17/5/39-14/8/39HG	19,663
27/3/42-18/4/42LS	61,643
4/9/44-20/9/44HG	68,420
2/6/47-25/6/47HS	56,116 Derby
13/1/48-11/2/48LO	13,119 Derby
29/8/49-29/4/49HG	47,417 Derby
17/12/51-14/1/52LI	45,419 Derby
26/7/54-19/8/54HG	52,118 Derby
10/8/57-27/8/57HI	57,877 Derby

47568 Sheds	
Low Moor	10/9/28
Farnley Jct	20/12/30

47568 Boilers	
No.7844	14/8/39
No.7839	20/9/44
No.10237	29/9/49
No.13300	19/8/54

47569

Built as 16652 at Hunslet Engine Co. 14th September 1928
Renumbered 7569 3/5/37; 47569 w/e 27/8/49
3/5/37 Standard radius springs fitted
13/7/57 Modified pistons for continuous blowdown valves
Withdrawn w/e 12/11/60

47569 Repairs	
3/2/31-20/2/31LS	40,351
6/12/33-21/12/33HS	46,940
15/4/37-3/5/37LS	72,650
10/12/38-22/12/38HG	33,471
11/11/41-25/11/41LS	71,696
25/3/44-12/4/44HG	55,583
31/12/46-1/2/47LS	56,968 Leeds
4/7/49-24/8/49HG	52,734 Derby
5/6/52-2/7/52LI	55,257 Derby
25/10/54-19/11/54HG	47,784 Derby
17/6/57-1/7/57HI	52,015 Derby

47569 Sheds	
Low Moor	14/9/28
Farnley Jct	21/2/31

47569 Boilers	
No.7895	22/12/38
No.10237	12/4/44
No.6859	24/8/49
No.13315	19/11/54

The first BRITISH RAILWAYS on the tanksides, as we've frequently seen, had an extra space for the emblem which was being devised at the time. When it appeared, it dawned that the new organisation's title was being repeated and the lettering disappeared when it was time to put on the emblem transfer. Here the latter is newly applied at Farnley Junction, with the lettering already looking tired. The number has been brightened up but there was of course no point in titivating the BRITISH RAILWAYS. A. Scarsbrook, Initial Photographics.

The look at last. 47569 is properly garbed at Derby MPD after a Heavy General on 25 November 1954. This Jinty was only ever based in Yorkshire so these trips to Derby were probably the only occasions it ventured out of the county. The lack of piping this side will be apparent – a hundred-odd engines 47667-47666 were steam brake only and did not require the distinctive vacuum ejector arrangement on the right-hand side. R.J. Buckley, Initial Photographics.

47570

Built as 16653 at Hunslet Engine Co. 15th September 1928
Renumbered 7570 19/7/37; 47570 w/e 6/8/49
13/5/44 Regulator handle extension
13/5/44 Fitting steel in lieu of copper boiler tubes
Withdrawn w/e 30/9/61

47570 Repairs	
29/6/31-28/7/31LS	45,118
18/12/33-6/1/34HS	82,499
22/6/37-19/7/37LS	77,067
29/11/38-12/12/38HG	26,674
19/9/41-11/10/41LS	66,871
2/5/44-13/5/44HG	58,770
31/3/47-10/5/47LS	63,410 Leeds
20/6/49-2/8/49HG	48,137 Derby
7/5/52-29/5/52LI	57,685 Derby
16/3/55-6/4/55HG	56,310 Derby
18/1/58-30/1/58HI	53,927 Derby

47570 Sheds	
Low Moor	15/9/28
Farnley Jct	28/7/31

47570 Boilers	
No.7893	12/12/38
No.7534	13/5/44
No.7334	2/8/49
No.13323	6/4/55

47571

Built as 16654 at Hunslet Engine Co. 19th September 1928
Renumbered 7571 8/4/37; 47571 w/e 4/6/49
15/12/33 Fitting clips for coal slacking pipe
Withdrawn w/e 13/5/61

47571 Repairs	
6/1/31-16/1/31LS	40,016
24/5/33-17/6/33LS	39,263
27/11/33-15/12/33HO	6,927
17/3/37-8/4/37LS	68,372
10/11/38-25/11/38HG	32,605
16/10/41-1/11/41LS	66,743
11/3/44-27/3/44HG	55,406
7/1/47-17/2/47HS	59,312 Leeds
4/5/49-1/6/49HG	44,430 Derby
30/7/51-23/8/51LI	47,880 Derby
31/3/54-30/4/54HG	52,823 Derby
29/1/57-12/2/57LI	51,593 Derby

47571 Sheds	
Low Moor	19/9/28
Farnley Jct	24/1/31
Wakefield	24/1/59
Accrington	31/12/60
Rose Grove	29/4/61

47571 Boilers	
No.7849	25/11/38
No.7890	27/3/44
No.13302	1/6/49
No.6874	30/4/54

47571 busies itself under the wires at Crewe, date unrecorded. It was transferred from Accrington to Rose Grove in April 1961 where withdrawal came after a few days. Maybe Crewe South kept it for a while and it never in fact got to the Burnley shed.

47572

Built as 16655 at Hunslet Engine Co. 24th September 1928
Renumbered 7572 1/6/37; 47572 w/e 15/5/48
19/2/44 Regulator handle extension
19/2/44 Fitting steel in lieu of copper boiler tubes
Withdrawn w/e 19/5/62

47572 Repairs	
13/8/31-16/9/31LS	45,147
1/1/34-20/1/34HS	37,893
11/5/37-7/6/37LS	71,506
20/1/39-26/5/39HG	37,301
23/12/41-17/1/42HS	55,853
1/1/44-26/1/44HG	54,200
17/9/45-2/10/45LS	46,807
14/4/48-11/5/48LS	64,076 Derby
8/1/51-26/1/51HG	57,018 Derby
18/4/55-10/5/55HG	92,879 Derby
9/6/58-19/6/58LI	71,233 Derby

47572 Sheds	
Low Moor	24/9/28
Farnley Jct	28/9/35
Agecroft	16/11/40
Wakefield	14/8/48
Goole	5/8/50
Wakefield	2/9/50
Lostock Hall	31/12/60

47572 Boilers	
No.7810	26/5/39
No.11875	26/1/44
No.13646	26/1/51
No.8089	10/5/55

47573

Built as 16656 at Hunslet Engine Co. 27th September 1928
Renumbered 7573 23/5/34; 47573 w/e 3/9/49
Withdrawn w/e 24/12/60

47573 Repairs	
24/3/31-16/4/31LS	42,033
9/4/34-23/5/34HS	46,825
10/2/37-26/2/37LS	59,403
24/5/39-18/9/39HG	51,879
19/5/42-6/6/42HS	68,778
26/8/44-9/9/44HG	63,061
16/6/47-23/8/47LS	79,064 Leeds
4/8/49-30/8/49HG	35,699 Derby
27/12/52-20/1/53HI	71,963 Derby
18/4/56-4/5/56HG	76,627 Derby

47573 Sheds	
Low Moor	27/9/28
Farnley Jct	18/4/31
Agecroft	16/11/48
Wakefield	14/8/48

47573 Boilers	
No.7834	24/5/39
No.6633	9/9/44
No.7826	30/8/49
No.13309	4/5/56

47574

Built as 16657 at Hunslet Engine Co. 3ʳᵈ October 1928
Renumbered 7574 4/3/36; 47574 w/e 23/10/48
18/11/33 Fitting clips to coal slacking pipe
30/10/43 Fitting steel in lieu of copper boiler tubes
Withdrawn w/e 15/12/62

47574 Repairs	
19/5/31-6/6/31LS	46,367
1/3/33-18/3/33LS	29,185
31/10/33-18/11/33HO	8,405
29/1/36-4/3/36LS	49,901
1/10/37-21/10/37LS	35,231
15/11/38-2/12/38HG	22,647
7/5/41-26/5/41LS	60,319
19/10/43-30/10/43HG	65,001
8/4/46-27/4/46HS	66,478
15/9/48-22/10/48HG	61,494 Derby
7/5/51-29/5/51LI	63,968 Derby
19/6/53-11/8/53HG	51,764 Derby
21/12/55-5/1/56LI	49,880 Derby
11/8/58-8/9/58HG	58,824 Derby

47574 Sheds	
Low Moor	3/10/28
Newton Heath	13/6/31
Agecroft	3/11/34

47574 Boilers	
No.7846	2/12/38
No.7855	30/10/43
No.7844	22/10/48
No.6863	11/8/53
No.10586	8/9/58

47575

Built as 16658 at Hunslet Engine Co. 9ᵗʰ October 1928
Renumbered 7575 20/12/35; 47575 w/e 21/5/49
6/2/34 Fitting clips to coal slacking pipe
25/12/43 Regulator handle extension
25/12/43 Fitting plate to bunker rails to prevent coal spillage
25/12/43 Fitting steel in lieu of copper boiler tubes
Withdrawn w/e 19/3/60

47575 Repairs	
22/7/31-8/8/31	
18/8/31-19/8/31LS	44,486
16/1/34-6/2/34HS	39,723
7/12/35-20/12/35LS	49,418
25/3/38-14/4/38LS	66,048
30/1/39-15/7/39HG	19,465
12/9/40-5/10/40LO	30,935
10/3/42-15/4/42HS	37,274
28/11/43-20/12/43HG	44,806
12/10/45-31/10/45LS	51,288
23/5/47-10/6/47LS	42,373 Derby
30/4/49-18/5/49HG	50,264 Derby
19/9/51-10/10/51LI	60,432 Derby
10/5/54-2/6/54HG	68,284 Derby

47575 Sheds	
Low Moor	9/10/28
Farnley Jct	5/9/31
Wakefield	24/2/34
Rose Grove	21/4/34
Stored unserviceable 26/4/58-19/3/60	

47575 Boilers	
No.7477	15/7/39
No.7837	20/12/43
No.6875	18/5/49
No.7173	2/6/54

47576

Built as 16659 at Hunslet Engine Co. 11ᵗʰ October 1928
Renumbered 7576 18/11/36; 47576 w/e 25/12/48
29/11/47 Fitting steel in lieu of copper boiler tubes
Withdrawn w/e 24/9/60

47576 Repairs	
2/1/31-16/1/31LS	39,329
18/1/33-3/2/33LS	54,650
9/5/34-25/6/34HG	34,490
12/10/36-18/11/36LS	59,383
27/10/39-11/11/39HG	65,101
2/9/42-1/10/42HS	85,179
24/12/43-15/1/44HG	30,826
25/10/45-16/11/45LS	55,954
15/1/47-6/2/47HS	35,144 Derby
15/11/48-24/12/48HS	50,394 Derby
5/12/50-1/1/51HI	47,828 Derby
3/8/53-30/9/53HG	60,137 Derby
2/3/56-19/3/56HI	51,090 Derby

47576 Sheds	
Low Moor	11/10/28
Farnley Jct	24/1/31
Accrington	21/2/31
Rose Grove	28/9/35
Newton Heath	20/8/60

47576 Boilers	
No.7334	27/10/39
No.7489	15/1/44
No.6835	6/2/47
No.7499	30/9/53

47577

Built as 16660 at Hunslet Engine Co. 20ᵗʰ October 1928
Renumbered 7577 18/9/37; 47577 w/e 21/8/48
7/9/57 Modified piston for continuous blowdown gear
Withdrawn w/e 27/3/65

47577 Repairs	
20/10/30-3/11/30LS	41,316
28/11/33-15/12/32LS	78,358
29/8/34-25/9/34HG	27,523
1/9/37-18/9/37HS	61,381
25/9/39-25/10/39HG	43,440
1/6/42-2/7/42LS	67,038
4/4/44-21/4/44HG	49,044
26/1/46-8/3/46HS	38,990
21/7/48-20/8/48HS	53,729 Derby
25/4/51-16/5/51LI	56,849 Derby
6/1/54-3/2/54HG	54,786 Derby
25/6/57-11/7/57LI	66,771 Derby
3/2/61-17/3/61HG	65,776 Derby

47577 Sheds	
Newton Heath	20/10/28
Farnley Jct	7/9/35
Wakefield	16/11/40
Newton Heath	6/12/47
Rose grove	21/8/54
Skipton	9/7/60
Lostock Hall	10/8/63
Fleetwood	27/2/65

47577 Boilers	
No.6823	25/10/39
No.7835	21/4/44
No.11552	20/8/48
No.14050	3/2/54
No.11883	17/3/61

47578

Built as 16661 at Hunslet Engine Co. 24th October 1928
Renumbered 7578 26/5/37; 47578 w/e 30/7/49
Withdrawn w/e 27/3/65

47578 Repairs	
28/10/30-6/11/30LS	43,486
31/5/32-24/6/32LS	74,271
10/7/34-14/8/34HG	57,813
27/4/37-26/5/37HS	61,749
31/5/38-10/6/38LO	21,145
25/1/40-19/2/40HG	48,388
8/10/41-8/11/41LS	39,686
19/10/43-2/11/43LS	55,430
29/7/44-24/8/44LO	21,089
21/3/45-31/3/45HG	15,220
8/10/47-3/11/47LS	63,399 Derby
13/6/49-27/7/49HG	41,325 Derby
18/12/51-10/1/52HI	64,255 Derby
25/6/54-6/8/54HG	61,509 Derby
23/5/57-10/6/57HI	58,546 Derby
14/3/60-22/4/60HG	51,625 Derby

47578 Sheds	
Newton Heath	24/10/28
Agecroft	4/1/36

47578 Boilers	
No.6843	19/2/40
No.7568	31/3/45
No.13310	27/7/49
No.12682	6/8/54
No.13972	22/4/60

7574 (47574) had been renumbered from 16657 in 1934; its re-painting would presumably date from the Heavy General of 1938. Rail Archive Stephenson.

16658 (7575, 47575) in the early 1930s. Lower roof rain strip not there yet. Location a puzzle; in the distance is what looks to be an engine shed roof but it doesn't ring a bell. Rail Archive Stephenson.

47577 at its then home Newton Heath, about 1948/49. The new front number plate is there and LMS is still visible despite some attention – whether to highlight it or expunge it is not clear; the bunker number is not visible though the assumption has to be that it is in fact there – rendered unseen by the angle of light perhaps. RailOnline

47579

Built as 16662 at Hunslet Engine Co. 1st November 1928
Renumbered 7579 11/8/37; 47579 w/e 9/7/49
11/8/37 Refitted with standard radius springs
Withdrawn w/e 4/7/64

47579 Repairs	
4/6/30-2/7/30LS	36,071
4/8/32-23/8/32LS	35,661
18/10/33-8/11/33LO	20,506
11/5/34-6/7/34HG	10,508
13/7/37-11/8/37HS	58,989
5/7/39-17/10/39HG	37,830
24/2/42-25/3/42HS	57,306
12/8/44-9/9/44HG	66,500
9/4/47-3/5/47HS	61,201 Derby
11/6/49-8/7/49HG	53,291 Derby
1/1/52-29/1/52HI	66,766 Derby
6/5/54-3/6/54HG	55,302 Derby
14/5/57-29/5/57LI	65,143 Derby
6/6/60-5/8/60HG	61,202 Derby

47579 Sheds	
Newton Heath	1/11/28
Agecroft	4/1/36

47579 Boilers	
No.7897	5/7/39
No.7485	9/9/44
No.13309	8/7/49
No.13295	3/6/54
No.14042	5/8/60

Below. 16661 (7578, 47578) could be anywhere, though the Lanky 0-6-0 in the background suggests somewhere north of a line from Chester to the Wash. Certainly it was only ever at ex-L&Y sheds. Rail Archive Stephenson.

Bottom. 47579 at Agecroft in the 1950s – the '11' would be a colliery 'target'. Whatever the year, it is definitely winter, with those coals going away in the brazier to protect the water column. The engine never really left Manchester, apart from runs to Derby for overhaul. RailOnline